Rhinegold Revision Guide

Lifelines
Edexcel A2 Music Technology
by
Chris Duffill and Rob Steadman

R·

Rhinegold Publishing Limited
241 Shaftesbury Avenue
London
WC2H 8TF
Telephone: 020 7333 1720
Fax: 020 7333 1765
www.rhinegold.co.uk

Rhinegold Music Study Guides
(series editor: Paul Terry)

Students' Guides to GCSE, AS and A2 Music for the AQA, Edexcel and OCR Specifications
Listening Tests for GCSE, AS and A2 Music for the AQA, Edexcel and OCR Specifications

A Student's Guide to GCSE Music for the WJEC Specification
A Student's Guide to Music Technology for the Edexcel AS and A2 Specification
Listening Tests for Students: Edexcel AS and A2 Music Technology Specification

The following books are designed to prepare for and support all GCSE and A-level music courses:
Key Stage 3 Listening Tests: Book 1
Music Literacy Workbook (for GCSE and A-level)
A Student's Guide to Harmony and Counterpoint (for AS and A2 Music)

Other Rhinegold Study Guides
A Student's Guide to AS Classical Civilisation for the AQA Specification
Students' Guides to AS and A2 Drama and Theatre Studies for the AQA and Edexcel Specifications
Students' Guides to AS and A2 Performance Studies for the OCR Specification
Students' Guides to AS and A2 Religious Studies for the AQA, Edexcel and OCR Specifications

Rhinegold Publishing also publishes Classical Music, Classroom Music, Early Music Today, Music Teacher, Opera Now, Piano, The Singer, Teaching Drama, British and International Music Yearbook, British Performing Arts Yearbook, Rhinegold Guide to Music Education, Rhinegold Dictionary of Music in Sound.

First published in 2007, new edition 2008, in Great Britain by
Rhinegold Publishing Ltd
241 Shaftesbury Avenue
London WC2H 8TF
Telephone: 020 7333 1720
Fax: 020 7333 1765
www.rhinegold.co.uk

© Rhinegold Publishing Ltd 2007, 2008

All rights reserved. No part of this publication may be reproduced, stored in a retrieval system, or transmitted in any form or by any means, electronic, mechanical, photocopying, recording or otherwise, without the prior permission of Rhinegold Publishing Ltd.

Rhinegold Publishing Ltd has used its best efforts in preparing this guide. It does not assume, and hereby disclaims, any liability to any party for loss or damage caused by errors or omissions in the guide whether such errors or omissions result from negligence, accident or other cause.

You should always check the current requirements of the examination, since these may change.
Copies of the Edexcel Specification may be obtained from Edexcel Examinations at
Edexcel Publications, Adamsway, Mansfield, Nottinghamshire, NG18 4FN
Telephone: 01623 467367, Fax 01623 450481, Email publications@linneydirect.com
See also the Edexcel website at www.edexcel.org.uk

Lifelines Edexcel A2 Music Technology
British Library Cataloguing in Publication Data
A catalogue record for this book is available from the British Library

ISBN: 978-1-906178-33-8

Printed in Great Britain by Thanet Press Ltd

Contents

Introduction 5
Controlling and Interpreting MIDI Data 6
Controlling and Interpreting MIDI Data: Questions 17
Controlling and Interpreting MIDI Data: Answers and Commentary 26
Music Technology in Context 44
Area of Study: Music for the Moving Image 47
Area of Study: Words and Music 60

THE AUTHORS

Chris Duffill has a background of 20 years experience in popular music recording, production and performance, as a keyboard player, arranger, composer and electronic musician. He developed skills and techniques in sound engineering, synthesis, sampling and sequencing on the job as the technology has advanced, and is at home with many styles from electronic dance to world, pop and rock. For the past six years he has expanded his involvement into education, developing provision of music technology at A level and across the curriculum, working as a teacher, training provider and course leader, and as a senior examiner for A-level Music Technology.

Rob Steadman is a composer and part-time teacher at Lady Manners School, Bakewell. He has written two symphonies, two operas, musicals, a number of choral works and a large amount of chamber music, including compositions for the Royal Philharmonic Orchestra, the percussionist Evelyn Glennie and the Holywell Ensemble, and together with author Richard Adams. He is a regular contributor to *Classroom Music* and has examined for all the major exam boards. His website is: www.robertsteadman.com.

ACKNOWLEDGEMENTS

The authors would like to thank Hugh Benham for his expert advice during the preparation of this book, and Paul Terry for his suggestions and corrections. Thanks also to Elisabeth Boulton, Sabine Wolf, Emma Findlow, Zöe Franklin, Nicola Goodman, Ben Robbins, Rosamund Spinnler and Lucien Jenkins of Rhinegold Publishing for their assistance throughout the editing and production process.

Chris Duffill would like to thank Dr Neil Day, David Ventura, Sally Ellerington, Nick Bristow, Rebecca Gretton, Charlotte Manners, Karen Treep and Beth Duffill for their support and assistance during the preparation of this book.

Introduction

For A2 Music Technology you have to complete the following coursework:
- Sequencing, Recording and Producing (30% of your total A2 mark)
- Composing Using Technology (30% of your total A2 mark).

And you have to sit two written papers:
- Controlling and Interpreting MIDI Data (25% of your total A2 mark)
- Music Technology in Context (15% of your total A2 mark).

This guide will help you revise for the two written papers.

During AS Music Technology you will have studied a variety of music from pop and jazz to music from the western classical tradition, as well as the use of technology in music production and performance. In A2 this study becomes more focused, and you will have studied two set works. This study will prepare you for the Music Technology in Context paper.

Depending on the option you or your teacher selected, you will have either studied the music from two films (*Goldfinger* and *Batman*) or two albums (The Who's *Who's Next* and Madonna's *The Immaculate Collection*).

The knowledge and skills you gained at AS are still important here, and need to be applied in the analysis and understanding of these works – you will still need to recognise musical features, and use technical and theoretical musical language to describe what is in the music.

The Controlling and Interpreting MIDI Data exam requires you to study three representations of the same piece of music: a live recording, a printed score and a MIDI file. You will have to analyse and compare these with a particular focus on the MIDI file, comparing its accuracy and effects to the other two versions. This is something you will need to practise because, as with all musical skills, practice makes perfect.

This *Lifelines* revision guide will help prepare you for these two written exams and ease the revision process – but, of course, the real work is down to you. It is important that you set aside sufficient time to work on the skills and knowledge required by the examiners and that you create a working environment without distractions. You must be familiar with the set works and confident using a sequencer.

Good luck and enjoy your revision!

A2 6718/01
Controlling and Interpreting MIDI Data

INTRODUCTION TO THE PAPER

This paper is one hour long, plus ten minutes reading time at the start. You will then complete the second written paper, Music Technology in Context [6718/02A or 02/B], also one hour long, on your chosen area of study (see page 44). There can be a short supervised break between the exams; if there are too few workstations for all students to sit this paper at the same time the order of the papers may be reversed for some of the group, or the start time may be staggered.

For the exam you have three representations of a piece of music: a recorded live performance, the full score, and a MIDI file interpretation. Using a computer workstation to listen to the audio file (through Windows Media Player, iTunes and so on) and playing the MIDI file in your sequencer (Cubase, Sonar, or Logic), you will have to analyse aspects of all three sources to show your knowledge and understanding of music notation, aural skills, recording, production and sequencing techniques.

You will be able to listen to the audio recording and MIDI file for a short period of no more than 30 seconds to check that they play back correctly on your system. You then have ten minutes of reading time to study the printed score and the questions. You will not be allowed to listen to the audio recording or MIDI file during this time, or examine the MIDI file in any way, or to write anything down.

During the hour you will have 11 questions to answer. All questions must be answered.

Section A consists of questions 1–5; these contain a mixture of multiple-choice and short-answer questions, in several parts, and relate to the score and the recorded audio version of the music. Each question is worth a variable number of marks, with a clear indication of what is required for each part of the question and the total marks for the complete question. The total for this section is 35 marks.

Section B is composed of questions 6–11; there is a mixture of short answers, tables to complete with values of data and explanations/reasons for their use, and occasionally multiple-choice answers. These examine your ability to analyse the MIDI-file performance, show your understanding of how sequencers and the associated technology (MIDI controller keyboards, General MIDI soundset) are used to create musical performance, and also the limitations that exist in this way of producing music. The total for this section is 65 marks.

The paper also tests your knowledge of two Areas of Study: Popular Music and Jazz; and Development of Music Technology. You need to be able to listen to music you may not have heard before and identify aspects of the music and the technology it employs.

The sample questions presented here are designed to be close to what you will have in the actual exam. The audio recording, MIDI file and score supplied with the *Listening Tests for Students for the Edexcel AS and A2 Music Technology Specification* (Rhinegold Publishing 2004) and CD, entitled *All In This Together*, are used for the materials needed to answer the questions.

> **Important note:**
> The MIDI file supplied on the CD (All In This Together.mid) has some omissions that may affect your ability to answer the questions supplied. Alternative versions are available on the Rhinegold website in the Lifelines support material section (All In This Together 2.mid or the Cubase native file All In This Together 2.cpr which is recommended for users of Cubase SX version 2 or higher). There is more detailed discussion of differences you will find between this MIDI file and the one supplied in your examination in the commentary starting on page 26, where the nature of the differences can be seen in context. Also, the MIDI file used for these questions probably has less of a variety of controllers and programming techniques than you will get in your exam, so you are advised to be aware of all the types of sequencing techniques outlined in the 'Techniques' and the 'Key Terms and Concepts' sections below.

Section A

Section A of this paper will include questions on various aspects of music theory, identified from the score and aurally through listening to the recording; you will be required to identify where a certain feature occurs, complete a rhythm on a stave, comment on key, use of harmony/chords and tempo. There will also be questions on recording and production, such as identifying and commenting on microphone and recording techniques, effects used, stereo field/panning, and use of electronic instruments. There will be questions on performance techniques and characteristics of the style, such as questions about the social and historical context of a given style or era. Some parts of questions may not be specifically about the material in the extract, but ask you to show general knowledge of something featured in the song.

Below is a list of the types of question that almost certainly will appear in section A:

- Identifying and explaining the use of various **musical symbols** and **instructions** in the score
- Identifying **chords** used at various points by analysing the score
- Commenting on **phrase structure** – how long the phrases are in a certain section and what kind of variations are used
- Other aspects of the music such as **texture, instrumentation, timbre, form**
- One or more questions on **recording technique** for a specific instrument/group of instruments such as acoustic guitar, saxophone or vocals. You will need to show awareness of **microphone choice and placement, room acoustics** and other factors involved in the recording, including possible difficulties
- You will be asked about **mixdown** and **production techniques** such as the use of **effects, EQ** and **dynamics processing**, as well as **level** and **stereo field** (use of pan).

8 Controlling and Interpreting MIDI Data

Section B

Section B asks questions on the MIDI-file performance, and you will need to show awareness of sequencing techniques:

- Methods of **data entry** (live performance, entry via key editor or step entry)
- Shaping **rhythm** using **quantisation** (hard/soft, manual editing of timing)
- Using **velocity** for **accenting/phrasing**
- Selecting and changing sounds – **General MIDI soundset**
- Other **General MIDI conventions** such as **reset** and **system exclusive** messages
- The full range of **MIDI controllers**, their uses and methods of entry/editing to create aspects of musical performance.

TECHNIQUES AND APPROACHES FOR SITTING THE EXAM

Giving yourself the best chance of success in the exam not only depends on ensuring your knowledge of the areas to be assessed is in prime condition, but also that you are able to do yourself justice by performing to the best of your ability.

Manage your time

If you think that one hour doesn't seem like a long time, then you're right, it isn't for this exam. The crucial factor is being able to work swiftly through the questions, getting straight to the required place in the score/recording and knowing where to find the sequencing techniques in the MIDI file.

During the hour of the exam you will have to answer questions worth a total of 100 marks, which works out at your needing to cover about ten marks every six minutes, so you will have to work through the questions at a fast pace. Allow yourself no more than 20 minutes for Section A, leaving 40 minutes for Section B.

You will have to listen to the audio file, following the score at first, then pinpointing exact areas of the score and recording that relate to the questions. When you have finished Section A, you will need to listen to the MIDI file in its entirety, then listen again focusing on smaller sections or using the solo function to isolate instruments as needed to answer questions.

The order in which you tackle the questions is up to you, but do follow the format of answering questions in Section A first and then move on to Section B. Section A prepares the way for analysing the MIDI file, and you will need to refer to both score and recording at times when answering questions in Section B. **In Section A there is no need to look at or listen to the MIDI file at all.**

Make sure you complete the questions that carry a lot of marks first; don't get bogged down over a question you find difficult which is only worth three or four marks.

The ten minutes reading time at the start offers you a valuable way to prepare for the work you will have to cover. You can look at the score and the questions; you can decide where in the score or recording you need to focus to answer questions in Section A. You may even be able to answer some of the questions relating to the score in your head. Look also at Section B questions carefully, and plan where in the MIDI file you will need to look to answer questions, which questions carry the most marks and which you can tackle confidently.

Using the equipment effectively

Firstly, make sure you have the headphones on the correct way round: the right earpiece is marked 'right' or 'R'. The type of headphones you use is important too. They need to be as accurate as possible, and in good condition, so the sound doesn't cut out or break up due to worn-out wiring. Small iPod-type headphones are best avoided, as they do not have an accurate frequency response. Hopefully, your centre will be able to provide you with decent headphones for the exam, probably ones that you are used to from your coursework, but it is even better if you have your own pair that you can get used to working with. Budget versions by reputable recording equipment manufacturers like Sennheiser, AKG or Beyerdynamic are worthwhile and inexpensive purchases.

You will use a computer-based media player to listen to the recorded audio file of the music in the exam; which one you use will depend on your centre's equipment. Make sure that all equalisers or tone controls are switched out; you need to hear the music as accurately as possible. A computer media player has the advantage that you can navigate quickly to any point in the song, to focus on a particular section that may need several listens, and see the time elapse clearly. You may have a pan control that allows you quickly to listen to one or other side of the stereo mix, which is useful for hearing the use of panning and also to focus on an instrument that is panned to one side if needed.

Know the correct answer, write the correct answer

- Always read the question carefully, making sure you understand precisely what is being asked.
- Follow the instructions on the front of the paper about how to write answers, for example in multiple-choice questions, the move to e-pen marking means answers must be indicated with a cross in a special box. If you need to change the answer, draw a horizontal line through the box.
- If you are really unsure, move on and avoid wasting time agonising over the right answer but make sure you attempt an answer before the hour has elapsed, even if it's a total guess.
- With multiple-choice questions, it's sometimes easier to see which answers are incorrect so they can be eliminated quickly.
- When written answers are required, pay attention to the number of marks given; there will usually be a clear indication of how many examples or points are required in the answer. For example, if you are asked to provide ideas for **two** challenges that are faced in recording a good acoustic guitar sound for example, there's no point in providing ten.
- The technical and musical vocabulary you use in written answers must be clear. There is a glossary and summary of concepts on page 11 to help you with this.

10 Controlling and Interpreting MIDI Data

Technique for answering the questions on the MIDI file

You will need to become very quick and efficient in negotiating your way around the various views/editors offered by your sequencer program. The front page gives you information on the tracks/instruments, timeline/bars, where note data and controller data are located in tracks (provided the correct view options are chosen). You can use the zoom in and out functions if necessary to see finer detail (this is more useful in editor windows).

The key editor (also called the piano roll or matrix editor in some programs) offers the most comprehensive level of detail. The notes are shown in relation to a MIDI keyboard and MIDI note numbers (C3, F#5 and so on), or drum sounds in the drum editor; note start times and lengths can be seen accurately, and the data lane at the bottom can be used to display velocity values (this is usually the default setting), or other values of MIDI controllers and data. There is a list of types of data and their musical application on pages 13–14 in the key technology terms and concepts section. You should become familiar with all the techniques, types of data and how they are used to create aspects of a musical performance.

You will be used to working with this editor from your sequencing and other coursework, so it may be that you just need to fine-tune your skills of interpreting all the different types of data on view. The list (or event) editor may be unfamiliar, but it also has its uses for this paper. Where single values of a MIDI controller are asked for, the list editor may be the best place to look. There are usually a number of single value controllers and other MIDI data at the start of the MIDI file, often volume, pan, effects send 1, expression, and program change. These will be positioned before the music starts, usually staggered so there is not a big logjam of data which can affect the playback of the sequencer and response of the General MIDI sound module.

> As discussed elsewhere, the MIDI file used for the questions in this book is missing some of the data you would expect to find at the start of a MIDI file.

The score (or staff) editor may be of use for identifying pitches, although be aware that it may display notes differently from the printed score (particularly note lengths) and you will need to set the key signature to the correct key as this may not have been done in the MIDI file.

There are always different view options, and therefore possibilities of changing what is displayed. You need to make sure that data you are searching for is not hidden or filtered by these settings. Hopefully the default settings in your sequencer will have everything displayed, but do take time to become familiar with how different views are displayed and hidden.

As well as the lists of key words and concepts below, there are detailed comments on the use of editors and MIDI data alongside the model answers, so you can see how the programs have been used to identify sources of information. Each sequencer package has its own peculiarities and differences. Some types of data may be easier to find or displayed in more places in each of the different packages, but it will be in there somewhere! Make sure you know how to find all the types of data in your particular sequencer. Make a list in the revision chart on page 16 to check that you can do this.

Apart from fine-tuning your knowledge and answer-writing technique, you need to make sure you are mentally and physically in a good state ready for the exam.

1. Rest is important; if you get nervous about exams then physical exercise can be an excellent way to unwind the day before. Listening to music is a great way to relax, but it may drive you crazy if you find yourself trying to analyse it rather than enjoying it.
2. The issue of food and drink is actually really important. Avoid sugary drinks and snacks as these make your energy and concentration levels dip after the initial rush. Make sure you have a good breakfast on the day of the exam. A bottle of water in the exam is a good idea.

KEY MUSIC TERMS AND CONCEPTS

Edexcel says that you need to be able to analyse music by listening or score-reading with reference to:

- Melody
- Harmony
- Rhythm
- Texture
- Timbre
- Form and structure
- Style (identifiers and history/social context)
- Performance techniques and characteristics.

There are many theory books, such as the *Music Literacy Workbook* (Rhinegold Publishing 2007), that cover this type of knowledge, and websites too, like www.musictheory.net. You can also use a score-writing program like Sibelius to test yourself on your knowledge of the various symbols.

The tools of the trade are scales, intervals, keys and key signatures, chords and chord patterns, note-length values, common and syncopated rhythms, tempo and time signatures, conventions of instrumental combinations, instrumental playing techniques, and common forms.

KEY TECHNOLOGY TERMS AND CONCEPTS

Microphones and recording technique:

- Understand the uses and conventions of the initial recording process
- Microphone types
- Pick-up patterns
- Positioning; close-microphone and ambient microphone use
- Room ambience and character
- Features of instruments to consider when recording
- DI technique
- Amps and pre-amps

12 Controlling and Interpreting MIDI Data

- Order of recording
- Overdub
- Double-tracking.

Electric and electronic instruments:
- Understand the way sound is created from a performance and technical perspective
- Electric guitars and basses
- Effects pedals
- Organs, pianos and other pre-synth electronic keyboards (for example clavinet)
- Analogue synths, polysynths, multitimbral synths
- FM synthesis
- Sampling
- S&S (sampling and synthesis, also known as ROMplers; this is the basis for sound card sounds and most multi-timbral modules)
- Modelling synths
- Drum machines
- Sequencers
- Electronic drums.

Mixing and production:
- Understand the approaches to refining and producing the finished product
- Level
- Pan
- EQ
- Compression
- Gating
- Reverb
- Delay
- Chorus
- ADT
- Flanger
- Phaser
- Distortion
- Lo-fi
- Production aims and approaches.

Sequencing:

i) Data entry methods
- Real-time performance from keyboard or other MIDI input device (drum pads, MIDI guitar/wind instrument)

Controlling and Interpreting MIDI Data

- Step-time entry
- Advantages and disadvantages of each.

ii) **Basic MIDI data**
- Note number (pitch)
- Start time (bars, beats, ticks)
- Length (duration, articulation)
- Velocity (accents and phrasing)
- Pitch-bend data/wheel (slides, melisma, string bend)
- MIDI channel (input and output)
- Program change number and name
- Tempo and tempo editor.
- Key signature/time signature settings and editor.

iii) **Editor windows**
- Types of data found in each editor window (Key editor AKA Piano Roll or Matrix; Drum Editor; List Editor AKA Event List; Score Editor AKA Staff View)
- Refining and shaping performance
- Techniques to create musical outcomes.

iv) **MIDI controllers; cc = continuous controller**
- Modulation Depth (cc1): adds vibrato, usually available via a modulation wheel or joystick on keyboards. (0 = no vibrato, 127 = maximum)
- Portamento Time (cc5): portamento is a smooth slide between pitches, used in conjunction with the 65 portamento on/off switch. This sets the rate of the slide; low values give a short slide time, higher values give a long slide time
- Main Volume (cc7): overall track volume, used to set relative levels of instruments in the mix. Available in console or mixer view as a slider, and on the main page of the sequencer for each track in its properties/inspector view
- Pan (cc10): stereo-field position (0 = far left, 64 = centre, 127 = far right)
- Expression (cc11): used to set changes in dynamics during a track
- Hold1 (damper) (cc64): sustain pedal. Notes will not receive a note-off message while this is active, so they will sustain indefinitely. Acts as a switch (values > 64 are on, < 64 is off)
- Portamento ON/OFF (cc65): used in conjunction with cc5, portamento time. Switches portamento on or off (values > 64 are on, < 64 is off)
- Filter Resonance (timbre/harmonic intensity) (cc71): a synthesis setting, controls how much emphasis is given to frequencies around the filter cut-off point
- Release Time (cc72): a synthesis setting, controls the length of time a sound lasts after the key has been released (tail of the ADSR amplitude envelope)
- Attack Time (cc73): a synthesis setting, controls the length of time a sound takes to reach its maximum amplitude after a key is struck (beginning of the ADSR amplitude envelope)

- Brightness (cc74): a synthesis setting, controls the filter cut-off point which is perceived as brightness (harmonic content)
- Reverb Send Level (cc91): controls how much signal is sent to the reverb unit built into the sound source (sound module, sound card synth)
- Chorus Send Level (cc93): controls how much signal is sent to the chorus unit built into the sound source (sound module, sound card synth)
- Reset All Controllers (cc121): returns all controller values to a default setting; for example pitch bend to 0, expression to 127, and lots more. Sent out at the start of a MIDI file by most sequencers. This controller sends on **all** MIDI channels – the others are only on their allocated channel.

ORGANISING YOUR REVISION AND USING YOUR TIME

Know the best way for you to work: plan in advance

- Everyone has preferences about how they work, when they work and how long they work. Some of us function better in the morning, some of us are more nocturnal, some prefer not to work straight after food. Knowing how you work best, when you are most alert and productive, will help you plan your study leave and revision time to the best effect.
- Don't over-exert yourself. It's often better to work for short periods with full concentration than force yourself to revise in long shifts.
- There is a chart on page 16 of this guide that you can fill in and use to help plan your revision work.

Answering exam questions: self-appraisal

At some point you should sit down with a complete set of questions, a music workstation, the audio recording, score and MIDI file, and one hour (plus ten minutes for reading) of uninterrupted time to complete the set of questions in this book. You should also work through other material using the *Listening Tests for Students for the Edexcel AS and A2 Music Technology Specification* (Rhinegold Publishing 2007) and past exam papers.

Your answers will form a record of where you have done well and where you need to improve, so you will need reflection time to analyse your answers carefully compared to the model answers. You could categorise the areas where you are successful, and those giving difficulties, so you have a list of where you need to direct your energy to improve performance.

You can also practise answering single questions using the time frame of six minutes for ten marks.

Improving listening skills

There are some tips in the commentary on the answers that can help you with listening skills; identifying pitches, intervals, rhythms, chords, and instruments. Communicating what you hear either in writing or on a stave is a skill that requires practice. Practise by listening to songs you know, as well as using the questions and model answers here; work out chord patterns so you recognise what different chord movements sound like, find the intervals used in the melody or riffs, work out the structure by counting bars in each section and naming the sections.

Play scales, intervals and chord patterns on your instrument to get used to hearing how they sound. Use a variety of keys. The same goes for identifying technology use, such as effects types, panning, and recording techniques. Practise identifying effect types in the studio by setting up reverbs, delays, and phasers with different settings and listening to them on one track of a recording, like a snare drum or vocal.

Knowledge of Areas of Study

Review the work done in your course. You will have studied many different aspects of music and technology during the two years. Use your notes, and your experience of the coursework, to reflect on this learning and to see just how much you have already developed your knowledge, listening and analysis skills.

Use the list of MIDI data and controllers to help you; you can check them off as you become confident in where to find them and ways to use them for musical results.

Like the answers to questions you have done, you can use these lists to focus on areas of strength and weakness. Make lists and plan for time to improve weaker areas.

Visual and aural aids to memory

Some concepts and facts that you find difficult to remember or grasp can be retained by making visual aids and sticking them on a wall where you will see them regularly. You could for example make a list of all the instruments that you would use a capacitor microphone to record, draw or find pictures of them and make a poster. You could also include information about positioning. Sometimes unusual or out-of-context images can be used as a memory trigger, such as an elephant next to a trumpet in the capacitor microphone uses list, which could indicate that this microphone must be used with care with the high sound pressure levels of a trumpet.

Aural aids could involve making short sequences that play different chord patterns and intervals, or you could program ring-tones on your phone that play an interval you find difficult to identify.

16 Controlling and Interpreting MIDI Data

Revision task	Materials needed	Time	Date	Targets for improvement
Answering questions				
Reflecting on answers				
Listening skills				
Music theory				
Production and recording				
Sequencing				

Controlling and Interpreting MIDI Data
Questions

SECTION A: ANALYSIS AND DISCRIMINATION

This section has questions relating to the score and recorded performance of the song. You can listen to the recording as many times as you wish. You will need to follow the score while listening, though the questions about the production will require close listening to the recording (please see note on page 7).

1. a) What key is this piece in? Underline your answer [1]

   G♯ minor   B major   F♯ major   C♯ minor

   b) Explain the meaning of the musical symbols shown below. Write your answers in the space provided in the table. [6]

Symbol	Part	Bar	Meaning
♩. = 65	All	1	
8va------ ⌐	Bass	3	
⁄⁄ (2 bar repeat)	Ac. Gtr	4 and 5	

Total 7 marks

2. Look at the drum part from bars 22–29.
   a) Which **two** bars are the same as each other, **though different from** bar 22? [2]

   ....

   b) Describe the phrase structure of the drums in this section of the song. [2]

   ....

   ....

   Total 4 marks

18 Controlling and Interpreting MIDI Data: Questions

3. a) Using standard chord symbols, such as C, Dmin, G7, write down which chords are playing at the points indicated in the song. [5]

Bar	Beat	Chord
14	1	
14	7	
15	1	
18	1	
22	7	

b) Which of the following is the correct chord symbol for the chord played in bar 18 beat 7? Underline your answer. [1]

C#7sus4   C#sus4   F#sus4   F#11

c) One of the instrumental parts is named 'Fender Rhodes'. Explain what this instrument is. [2]

....

....

Total 8 marks

4. This song is an example of indie music.
   a) List **three** features of the performance that support this statement. [3]

   I ....

   ....

   II ....

   ....

   III ....

   ....

   b) i) Which of the following bands/artists would you consider to be most similar in style to this recording? [1]

   Pink Floyd   The Beatles   Stone Roses   Robbie Williams

   ii) In what decade do you think this song was recorded? [1]

   ....

Total 5 marks

5. a) The Hammond organ in this recording uses a rotary speaker effect. Rotary speakers have a pair of treble speakers at the top, which can rotate at varying speeds, and a rotating drum at the bottom that acts on the bass speaker, creating a deep tremolo effect. The sound emerges from all four sides of the cabinet as the speakers rotate.

   i) Which other instrument in the recording uses this effect? [1]

   ....

   ii) Explain how you would set up a recording of an instrument using a rotary speaker. Your answer should indicate knowledge of microphone type(s) and placement, and reasoning for your choice in terms of how the sound can be used in the final mix. [3]

   ....

   ....

   ....

   ....

   ....

   iii) Describe one problem that could be encountered when recording a rotary speaker, and a strategy you would use to avoid or overcome this issue. [2]

   Problem: ....

   ....

   Strategy: ....

   ....

b) List **two** tracks on the recording where each of the two following effects or processing has been used. [4]

   Compression I ....

   II ....

   Reverb I ....

   II ....

c) What is the effect heard at 2:40–2:44? Underline your answer. [1]

   Digital delay   Flanger   Chorus   Saturated tape delay

Total 11 marks

Section A total 35 marks

SECTION B: CONTROLLING AND INTERPRETING MIDI DATA

You will need to focus on the MIDI-file performance of the song for this section, and use your sequencing program's various editor windows to obtain information asked for. You will also need to refer to the score at times, and the recording, when asked to compare elements of the performance between the MIDI file and the live version.

6. Program Change Events select the sound from the General MIDI soundset that will play on a particular track.

    a) Complete the table below, showing the program change numbers **and** program names for the tracks listed. [4]

Track name	MIDI channel	Program Change Number	Program Name
Backing Vcls	4		
Lead Vocals	5		
Fender Rhodes	6		
Hammond	7		
		½ mark x 4	½ mark x 4

    b) Why does each of these sounds need a different MIDI channel? [1]

    ....
    ....
    ....

    c) The Bass Guitar track could be described as wooden or mechanical, lacking in feel.

       i) List **two** reasons why this is the case. [2]

       I ....
       ....
       II ....
       ....

       ii) Explain how you could approach creating this bass part to avoid these problems. [2]

       ....
       ....
       ....
       ....

Total 9 marks

7. a) Analyse the Lead Vocal track between bars 14 and 48. Identify errors in pitch using the table; one line has been completed as an example. [10]

	Bar number	Beat	Correct Pitch in Score	Incorrect Pitch in MIDI file
Example	16	1	G♯	D♯
1				
2				
3				
4				
5				
	5 x 1 mark		5 x 1 mark	

b) There is also an error in the Lead Guitar track between bars 14 and 48 compared to the performance and the score, though not in pitch. Explain what the error is and in which bar(s) it occurs. [2]

Error: ....

....

Bar(s): ....

Total 12 marks

8. Study the Acoustic Guitar track and the Acoustic Gtr Dble track.
   a) i) List the values for controller 64, and which beat they occur on during bar 2 in the table below. [3]

Beat	Controller 64 value
½ x 3 marks	½ x 3 marks

   ii) Explain what aspect of the musical performance is being recreated using controller 64. You should refer to how the sound is changed and why the data is positioned as it is. [3]

....

....

....

   iii) Where else is controller 64 data used in the Acoustic Guitar track? [1]

....

22 Controlling and Interpreting MIDI Data: Questions

iv) What would the result be to the sound of the part if the data values for controller 64 in Track 3 were all changed by a value of 20? [2]

....

....

....

b) List **two** other programming techniques that have been used on the Acoustic Guitar track to recreate the performance of a real guitar. [2]

I ....

II ....

c) i) Why are the two acoustic guitar parts (Acoustic Guitar and Acoustic Gtr Dble) slightly offset in time? [1]

....

ii) Identify **two** ways the different acoustic guitar parts have been programmed to allow them to stand out from each other in the mix. [2]

I ....

II ....

Total 14 marks

9. a) i) List the pan values for each of the tracks named in the table below. [7]

Track	Pan value
Lead Guitar	
Electric Guitar	
Backing Vocals	
Lead Vocal	
Fender Rhodes	
Hammond	
Bass	

ii) Use the table below to illustrate how the Toms listed are panned by listening to the Drum part in bar 29, choosing from the following options:
- Hi Tom
- Low-Mid Tom
- Low Tom
- Floor Tom. [2]

Left	Centre	Right

iii) The Drum track is panned in the centre. Explain how the Toms have been made to pan across the stereo field. [2]

....

....

Total 11 marks

10. a) State the controller number and function of each of the MIDI controllers listed below. [4]

Name	Number	Function
Effects Depth 1		
Main Volume		

b) Comment on the settings that are used for these two controllers in this MIDI file, and how they could be changed to improve the mix. [2]

....

....

....

....

c) Identify the bar in the Drum track where there is a mistake in the values for Effects Depth 1, and explain what the mistake is. [2]

Bar: ....

Mistake: ....

....

Total 8 marks

24 Controlling and Interpreting MIDI Data: Questions

11. a) Use the table below to show how the MIDI file programmer has used sequencing techniques to emulate the performance techniques listed. An example is provided. [14]

Bar numbers in score	Track	Musical feature	Sequencing techniques used to emulate musical performance
6–7	Hammond	Decrease in volume	Controller 7 (main volume) is used to lower the volume gradually during the held chord in bar 6, as a volume pedal on an organ would do. The shape of the data is smooth rather than a sudden jump; this may have been achieved with a foot pedal or drawn in with the draw tool. The volume is returned to its previous value at the start of bar 7, where the Hammond is not playing, ready for the when it enters next.
14–18	Electric Guitar	Tremolo	
29–30	Fender Rhodes	Sustain pedal	
26–30	Electric Guitar	Change in tone/ pick up or amp setting	
36	Electric Guitar	Slide	

40	Bass	Grace note	
54–57	Lead Guitar	Hammer on	
74–end	All tracks except Electric Guitar	Fade at end	
			2 marks x 7

Total 14 marks

Section B total 68 marks

Controlling and Interpreting MIDI Data

Answers and Commentary

SECTION A: ANALYSIS AND DISCRIMINATION

1. a) F# major [1]

> Being able to identify the key chord of a song through listening is an important skill. You will need to be able to recognise key signatures to help with this, but remember they can be major or minor.

   b)

	Part	Bar	Meaning
♩. = 65	All	1	Play at a tempo of 65 beats per minute. Each beat is a dotted crotchet because the time signature is 12/8 (four groups of three quavers per bar). [2]
8va⁻⁻⁻⁻⁻┐	Bass	3	Play the notes one octave higher than written. [2]
𝄎	Ac. Gtr	4 and 5	Repeat the previous two bars. [2]

> *Any* musical symbols and performance instructions found on scores could be tested in this question.

Total 7 marks

2. a) Bar 25 and bar 27 [2]

   b) The drum part has a two-bar phrase structure in this eight-bar section; the first of each pair of bars is the same, with variations in the second bar including the Tom part in bar 29 which marks the end of the section. [2]

Total 4 marks

3. a) [5]

Bar	Beat	Chord
14	1	E
14	7	Emaj7
15	1	E7
18	1	F#
22	7	C#

> You will need to be able to identify chords from the notes in the score. You can practise this easily enough, reading pitches from bass and treble clefs and recognising basic major and minor triads and their extensions.

b) C♯7sus4 [1]
c) Any of: Fender Rhodes is an electric keyboard, used extensively in rock, jazz, soul and many other styles of music from the 1960s onwards. It is much favoured by piano players because of the weighted action keyboard, which is like a real piano rather than a synthesiser, and the characteristic timbre, which has a very warm, expressive and playable quality. [2]

Total 8 marks

4. a) I The prominent use of guitars, both strummed acoustic and electric lead. [1]
   II Emotional, sensitive rather than aggressive performance, notably in vocals, though still with 'attitude' and an edge. [1]
   III Care and attention to song writing and composition; reasonably detailed variations in structure, instrumentation and harmony without becoming over-complicated, mirroring approach of classic songwriters such as Bob Dylan or Lennon and McCartney. [1]
   b) i) Stone Roses [1]
      ii) 1990s [1]

Total 5 marks

5. a) i) The electric guitar (starting at 0:44). [1]
   ii) **Either:** By using two good-quality condenser (capacitor) microphones as a stereo pair, at either side of the cabinet at a distance between 20 cm and 30 cm. This will spread the rotary effect across the stereo field at mixdown. The height of microphones can be adjusted to capture more or less of the treble frequencies – the nearer the height is to the top of the cabinet the more prominent the treble speaker signal will be. [2]
   Or: a pair of good-quality condenser (capacitor) microphones, one positioned to capture the treble speaker at the top, at a distance of between 20 cm and 30 cm, and another at the same distance to capture the bass speaker. This will allow relative amounts of bass and treble speaker signals to be balanced at mixdown. The microphones should be placed on the same side of the cabinet to avoid phase problems. [2]
   iii) **Either:** Problem: wind noise from the rotating speaker as air is displaced. [1]
   Strategy: use a pop shield to minimise impact of wind noise; avoid pointing microphone directly at speakers (especially treble) or being too close. [1]
   Or: Problem: mechanical noise from motors and speaker rotation. [1]
   Strategy: make sure the instrument and amplifier are putting a healthy signal level into the speaker; mechanical noise is a constant level when it occurs, so the louder the instrument volume the less impact this noise will have. Make sure motors are in good condition and moving parts oiled as appropriate. [1]
   b) Compression: Any **two** from lead vocal, snare, bass drum, bass guitar. [2]
   Reverb: Any **two** from lead vocal, backing vocals, snare, toms, acoustic guitar, electric guitar, Hammond, Fender Rhodes **not** bass guitar or bass drum. [2]
   c) Saturated tape delay [1]

Total 11 marks

Section A total 35 marks

28 Controlling and Interpreting MIDI Data: Answers and Commentary

SECTION B: CONTROLLING AND INTERPRETING MIDI DATA

Important note: the MIDI file supplied for use with this question does not contain program 'change messages' embedded at the start of the MIDI tracks. The piece you have in the exam will contain these messages.

6. a)

Track name	MIDI channel	Program Change Number	Program Name
Backing Vocals	4	66 (65)	Alto sax
Lead Vocals	5	23 (22)	Harmonica
Fender Rhodes	6	6 (5)	E. Piano 2
Hammond	7	17 (16)	Drawbar organ
		½ mark x 4	½ mark x 4

All the questions in this section require you to be able to select and interpret data used in the MIDI file using the various views of your sequencer. Different sequencers have similar editing windows, and you will need to be fast and confident in your choice of where to find data in order to complete the questions in the time given. There are always several places where data appears, you will need to choose the option that is quickest and gives the required level of detail. You will also need to use zoom functions to focus on the wider overview or narrow detail.

Program change numbers can be found in the track properties area, or the track inspector for individual tracks. They will also appear as events in the list editor, and as a controller lane in the key editor.

The quickest way to view these in Sonar is in the Console window, where all the values can be seen together. See the examples on the next page.

Cakewalk Sonar

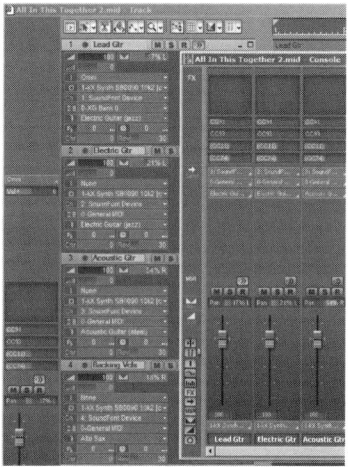

To select the Console view click on the View menu and select Console. Alternatively press <ALT> and <3> or click on the shortcut button next to DXi Synth Rack.

Note that program change numbers may not always appear, depending on the instrument selected in Options > Instruments. Here the XG set is used which displays the name and number; the GM and GS options only display the name.

The track inspector on the left-hand side provides an alternative, but this means that you can only look at each track individually.

Cubase and Sonar

In Cubase the track inspector on the far left is the best way to see this data, stepping through each track needed. If your set up only shows program numbers, like the example right, you will have to look elsewhere for the program names.

With a GM device selected in MIDI device manager (see below) you have data for patch numbers and names in view.

Notice how different programs use different terminology in places. For example, Sonar refers to program change numbers as 'patch change events'. Also the list of General MIDI program (or patch) names may be slightly different according to your sequencer and soundcard/ sound module. An example is patch 6, E. Piano 2, which may appear as Rhodes or Chorused Piano in other examples though it is the same sound. Even more confusing is the fact that Cubase and Sonar report different program change numbers! This is because Cubase numbers 0–127, while Sonar goes 1–128. This numbering system is equivalent since MIDI data always has 128 possible values.

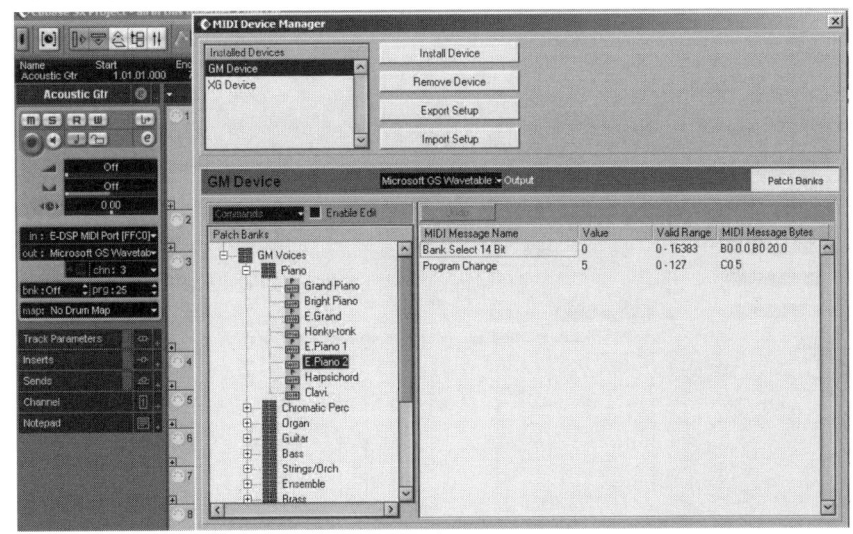

30 Controlling and Interpreting MIDI Data: Answers and Commentary

b) Each MIDI channel plays only one program/patch. If two tracks have the same MIDI channel but different program change numbers, they will both play the same sound which could be either of the selected patches. [1]

c) i) I: The part is tightly quantised, so that the note starts are all exactly, mathematically perfect. People play with more variation than this; even if they are incredibly tight rhythmically there will be slight variation to the rigid timing shown here. [1]

II: The velocities are nearly all at maximum, again giving no sense of emphasis to different notes in the phrases in the way a real player would do. [1]

ii) Playing the bass part in from a MIDI keyboard would give a more human feel, and in the editing stages if quantising is needed use soft or partial quantise settings to retain some variety to the timing (Cubase calls this 'iterative quantise'). Likewise with the velocity settings, which would be more natural with a real performance; these could be edited if necessary so that the important beats in the phrase are emphasised. [2]

Total 9 marks

The place for analysis of the performance of individual parts, as required in this type of question, is the Key editor (Cubase), Piano Roll editor (Sonar) or Matrix (Logic). Use solo to hear the part in isolation, or with drums to get an impression of how they work together.

You will be used to using this from your sequencing coursework, and you should be on the lookout for typical indicators of mechanical performance, such as over-quantisation and lack of variety in note length or velocity.

If necessary, examine individual note data to see start times and velocity values.

Sonar

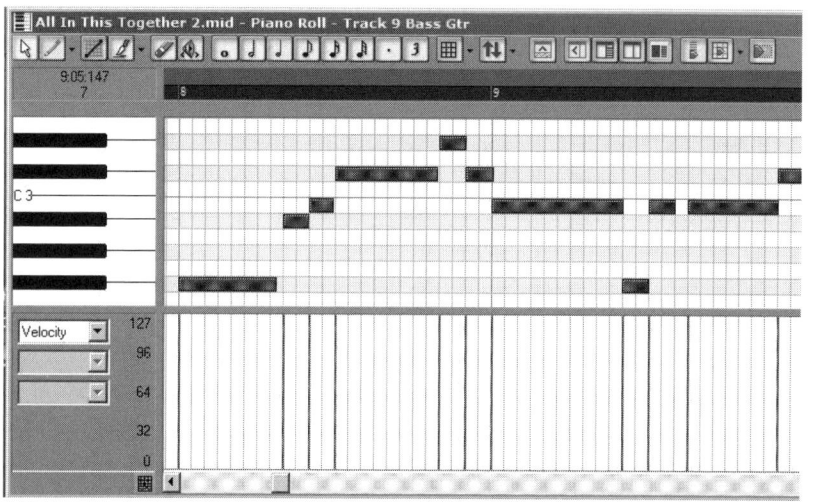

Controlling and Interpreting MIDI Data: Answers and Commentary 31

Cubase

Start times and velocity values are displayed as a list above the bar numbers for a selected note.

Note: Sonar uses a right click to display the note properties box.

7. a)

	Bar number	Beat	Correct Pitch in Score	Incorrect Pitch in MIDI file
Example	16	1	G#	D#
1	23	2	D#	A♮
2	27	1	D# (2nd 1/16th note)	B
3	27	2	D# (2nd 1/16th note)	B
4	31	11	C#	A♮
5	35	1	A#	G♮
	41	4	F#	E
others	44	1	A#	C#
	46	7	G#	D♮
	5 x 1 mark		5 x 1 mark	

b) Error: Note lengths become very short (staccato) when they should be legato. [1]
Bar(s): 40 and 41. [1]

Total 12 marks

Finding errors in the pitch is a listening exercise. Use solo to isolate the Lead Vocal part and listen while following the printed score. It may help to have the Score Editor window open to identify the pitch of the incorrect notes, though there are a few things to be aware of:

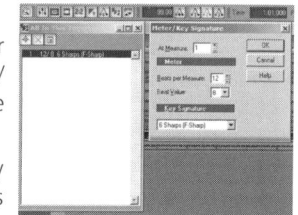

- The key signature may need to be set, or the score will appear very different. In Sonar (right) this is done from the Meter/ Key Signature dialog box. In Cubase this is set from the Score > Staff Settings dialog.

  Note: In Sonar this box also provides a list of key signatures with their names and number of sharps/flats – may be useful if you are unsure of a key and you need to identify it.

- Not all note lengths or rests will be displayed as they appear in the printed score, although they are the same in actual length. There is an example at the start of bar 26 below, where the C♯ at the end of bar 25 is slightly too long.
- The display resolution (display quantise in Cubase) must be set to the length of the shortest note – in this case a 1/16th note – or note lengths will be incorrect in places.

Alternatively, the Key Editor can be used to identify the pitches of individual wrong notes once they have been found by listening, using the methods described earlier to find the data on individual notes.

8 a) i)

Beat	Controller 64 value
1	127
7	0
7	127
3 x 1/2 marks	3 x 1/2 marks

ii) Controller 64 is a sustaining device, which has the effect of allowing notes to continue to resonate for as long as the sustain is on. This aims to recreate the ringing of acoustic-guitar strings when they are strummed. The data stops after the last strum on each chord, which lasts for half a bar (6 beats), and is then set to start again on the first strum of the next chord. [3]

iii) Used widely throughout the whole performance. [1]

Controlling and Interpreting MIDI Data: Answers and Commentary

    iv) The sound would not change, as controller 64 acts as an on/off switch. Values greater than 63 set the sustain to on, less than 63 switch it off. [2]

b) i) The notes are offset or staggered in each chord; with a down strum, the lower-pitched notes start earlier; with an up strum the higher-pitched ones do. [1]

    ii) The velocity of the first chord in every six strums (3 beats) is higher than the rest to give the kind of emphasis a guitarist would use. [1]

c) i) Offsetting the time gives a thicker sound to the identical parts (a bit like chorusing), and also recreates the slight timing variations that would occur between two performers. [1]

    ii) I: They use different programs/patches (steel string guitar and nylon guitar). [1]

       II: They are panned to opposite sides of the stereo field. [1]

Total 11 marks

When asked for a list of data values, the List/Event Editor can often be the best place to look. You can use the filtering function to remove the data you don't want to see; there will be lots of notes that can get in the way of viewing all the data you need to see.

Remember to uncheck the filtering function before you leave the editor window or it may confuse you next time!

Sonar uses a series of buttons to filter various data types:

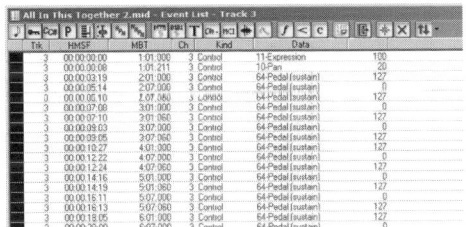

Cubase uses a number of check boxes:

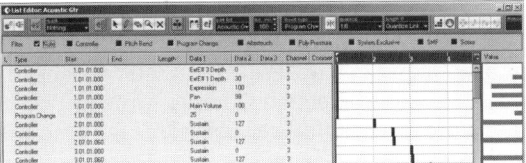

Both appear above the main data lists.

Note: Cubase does not show the controller number, only the name. The number appears when the controllers are viewed in the Key Editor.

34 Controlling and Interpreting MIDI Data: Answers and Commentary

Note: Controller 64 sustain has to be selected from the pop-up list to show the values in the controller lane at the bottom of the Key Editor window. In Cubase (below) you can see multiple lanes, whereas Sonar allows only one. Cubase also usefully displays a star next to controllers that are used in the track.

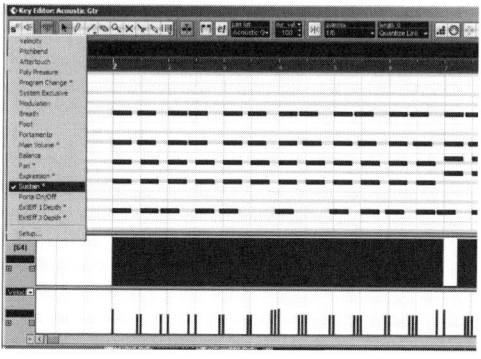

9. a) i) [7]

Track	Pan value
Lead Guitar	17%L or 52
Electric Guitar	21%L or 49
Backing Vocals	18%R or 74
Lead Vocal	20%L or 50
Fender Rhodes	34%R or 85
Hammond	20%R or 76
Bass	C or 64

See text box overleaf for explanation of different ways to show pan values.

ii) [2]

Left	Centre			Right
Floor Tom	Low Tom	Low-Mid Tom		Hi Tom

iii) Each individual Drum can have its own pan setting within the program/patch. The convention is to arrange Toms as a listener would hear them; these values are loaded automatically as default values in a General MIDI drum kit. [2]

Total 11 marks

Controlling and Interpreting MIDI Data: Answers and Commentary

In part a) there are several different ways of expressing pan values. Some programs show them as a percentage to the left or right (Sonar track properties/inspector), Cubase inspector shows [–]63 to [+]64 with 0 as centre or as a number from 0–127 with 64 in the centre (usually in the list editor).

Note for Cubase users: the correct values of pan were not displayed in this part of the program on the MIDI file provided with the Rhinegold Listening tests CD, using Cubase SX version 2.2. An alternative version, *All In This Together 2.mid* or the Cubase native file *All In This Together 2.cpr* can be downloaded from the Lifelines support material section on the Rhinegold website.

In part c) you need to show your knowledge of how the General MIDI soundset is configured. You could be asked anything about the conventions of General MIDI.

10. a)

Name	Number	Function
Effects Depth 1	91 [1]	Sets the amount of reverb send for an individual track and is used to set different reverb levels for tracks in the mix. [1]
Main Volume	7 [1]	Sets the overall volume for a track and is used to balance track levels in the mix. [1]

    b) These settings are all at the same value on each track (100 for main volume, 30 for Effects Depth 1). Changing the Main Volume levels would improve the balance of the mix, in particular the Lead Vocal could be more prominent and both Acoustic Guitars a bit quieter. Changing effects depth 1 levels would create a more realistic use of reverb, for example the backing vocals would benefit from more reverb and the main vocal slightly less. [2]

    c) Bar: 38 [1]

       Mistake: The value suddenly jumps to maximum, for no real reason. Sometimes a sudden increase in reverb can be used as production technique to emphasise a drum hit, but in this case it appears random. [1]

36 Controlling and Interpreting MIDI Data: Answers and Commentary

Main Volume and Effect Send 1 are important controllers that are used to create the finished mix of the piece of music, rather than being related to the musical performances themselves. Also included in this area are pan values (as looked at in Q9), and Effect Sends 2, 3, 4, if used.

These values can be seen in **Sonar** in the inspector (if the correct views are selected) and track properties area of the main sequencer window.

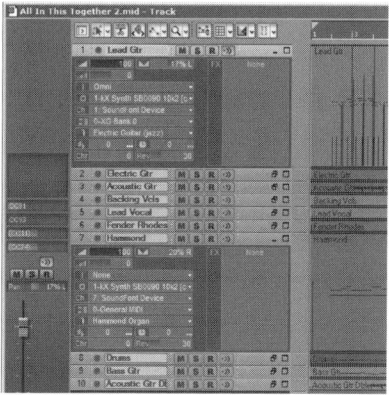

In **Cubase** the Main Volume is shown as well as pan.

The console or mixer view can also be used to display these values for all tracks (see question 6).

Important: in the exam there will also be an initial value for Main Volume, pan, Effects Send 1 at the start of each track in the MIDI file, though they are not included with the file supplied on the Rhinegold Listening Tests CD. The alternative files on the Rhinegold website in the Lifelines support material section *All In This Together 2.mid* or the Cubase native file *All In This Together 2.cpr* have the pan values entered at the start of each track. Expect different levels for these aspects of the mix in your exam; it would be unusual for all the values to be the same.

Controlling and Interpreting MIDI Data: Answers and Commentary

Total 8 marks

11.

Bar numbers in score	Track	Musical feature	Sequencing techniques used to emulate musical performance
6–7	Hammond	Decrease in volume	Controller 7 (main volume) is used to lower the volume gradually during the held chord in bar 6, as a volume pedal on an organ would do. The shape of the data is smooth rather than a sudden jump; this may have been achieved with a foot pedal or drawn in with the draw tool. The volume is returned to its previous value at the start of bar 7, where the Hammond is not playing, ready for the when it enters next.
14–18	Electric guitar	Tremolo	Rapid fluctuation in main volume, controller 7. The volume goes from a high value to a value just below half way with about 3 cycles per 1/8th note. This could have been entered using the draw tool or from a MIDI controller keyboard during live recording.
29–30	Fender Rhodes	Sustain pedal	The sustain pedal (controller 64) has a single value of maximum just after the start of bar 29, and a second value of 0 at the start of bar 30 when the Rhodes part has stopped. The sustain controller acts as an on/off switch and there are no varying amounts of sustain between 0 and 127, since it is either on or off like a sustain pedal on a piano which lifts the dampers off the strings. This could have been entered using an external pedal during live performance or written using the draw tool.
26–30	Electric Guitar	Change in tone/pick up or amp setting	The patch is changed using program change number at bar 26 beat 1, to electric guitar (clean) for the section of quiet 1/16th notes in the score. This has quite a thin sound. It is changed to electric guitar (jazz) at the end of bar 29 (during beat 12), which has a fatter sound for the tremolo part. This is also the patch used at the start of the track.
36	Electric Guitar	Slide	Pitch bends up a whole tone halfway through the C♯ to move to D♯ (where the note changes in the score). The pitch bend wheel remains on maximum during the following note, an E♮ in the score but a D♯ in the MIDI file. The pitch bend is then returned to zero quickly in the space between the E and the next note.

Controlling and Interpreting MIDI Data: Answers and Commentary

40	Bass	Grace note	The pitch bend up a tone is used from the maximum down value to the zero (central) position. This occurs quickly at the start of the D♯ on beat 10 of bar 40. This was probably entered using the pitch bend wheel in live performance, but could also have been done using the draw tool.
54–57	Lead Guitar	Hammer on	Pitch bend up is used from zero (central) position either to maximum or halfway depending on whether a whole tone or semitone is needed according to the score. It is always an almost instant change from zero to the final value. It always occurs halfway through the first note in every group of 6 beats, it remains on throughout those notes since the only time it can be returned to zero is at a break in the end of the 6 beats so the articulation remains legato. This means the rest of the notes have to be played not at the written pitch but at a pitch lowered by a semitone or tone as appropriate.
74–end	All tracks except Electric Guitar	Fade at end	Controller 11 expression is used to gradually lower the volume of all tracks, going from maximum (127) to zero over five bars. It is drawn in using the pencil tool, as the ramp is not completely smooth. Using the line tool would have given a completely smooth ramp. The first track values were probably copied and pasted to the other tracks to make the job easier and ensure that everything gets quieter at the same rate.
			2 marks x 7

Total 14 marks

Controlling and Interpreting MIDI Data: Answers and Commentary

Observe that the answers in the table all describe how the controller values and MIDI performance change during the music. Controllers nearly always have a shape according to how the data is entered: ramps, smooth curves, sudden jumps. Each of these will produce different results.

Checklist to describe MIDI controllers:

- Name the controller and give its number.
- What and where is the starting value?
- What and where is the ending value?
- How does it change in between?
- What musical function does the MIDI controller have when used in this way? (The same controller can have different results depending on how it is used, such as pitch bend and sustain in this MIDI file.
- Which data-entry methods have been used to get the controller information into the performance?

Often this information is best viewed in the Key Edit page, looking at the controller lane and observing the shape of the data while seeing the detail of where the notes fall. However, the list editor can help you determine exactly which controller is being used if you are unsure initially.

Make sure you have read the notes in the earlier section about the content and programming techniques in this MIDI file. You will have other techniques to answer questions on in your exam, such as different methods of note data entry (for example unedited live performance – the parts here are all heavily quantised), approaches to quantisation (hard/soft), velocity shaping though live performance and/or editing to give realistic phrasing and accenting, other controllers such as portamento and modulation, different uses of controllers shown here (no 11 expression to shape dynamics) and other aspects of MIDI file programming such as reset and systems exclusive data.

40 Controlling and Interpreting MIDI Data: Answers and Commentary

Hammond: volume pedal

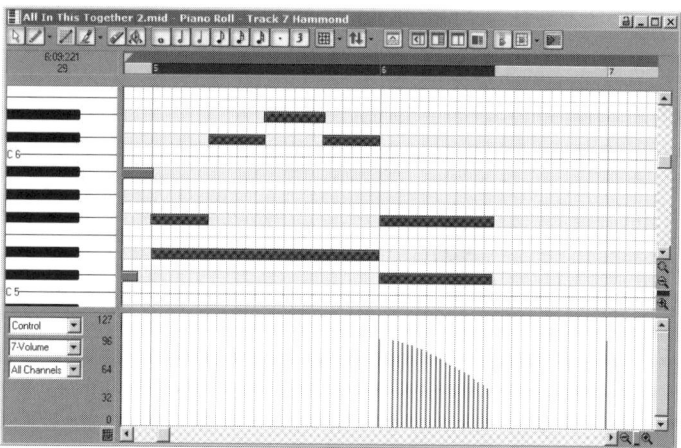

Note that the return to original value must be entered where nothing is playing or it will affect the note(s) that are sounding. Ramp-shaped data can be entered using the line tool for a straight ramp, or draw/pencil tool for a curved ramp though Cubase has the option of selecting curves with the line tool.

Important note for Sonar users: the controller data will not appear if the wrong channel is selected in the drop-down menu on the bottom left of the editor. This can be set at all channels to avoid this problem.

Electric guitar: tremolo

The uneven nature of the events and the fact that there are several values for high and low volume, plus the irregular timing of controller events, suggest that this may have been entered using an external volume knob or slider on a MIDI controller keyboard. It could also have been entered using a draw/pencil tool.

Fender Rhodes: sustain pedal

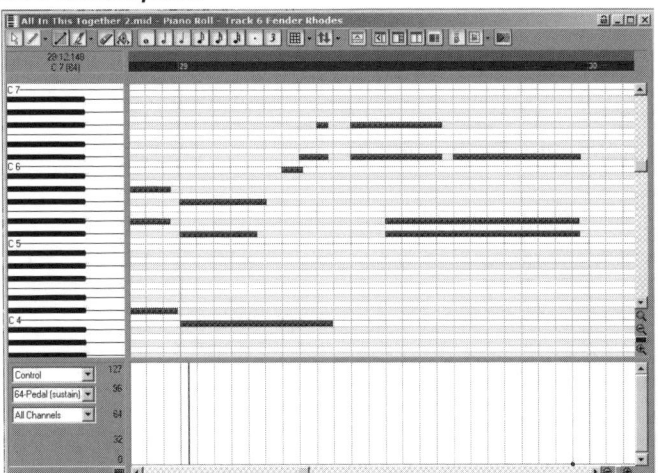

The single maximum and minimum values are all that is required since the sustain pedal controller acts as an on/off switch.

- Controllers that have an on/off action like this are called switch controllers.
- Controllers that have incremental values which gradually change the action according to higher/lower settings) are called continuous controllers.

Electric guitar: change in tone/pick up or amp setting

This is shown here in the List Editor window, with all note, pitch bend and controller events filtered out.

For Sonar users, patch/program change events are not shown as a controller lane in the Key Edit page. For Cubase users, program change numbers are shown as a controller lane in the Key Edit page. This is useful for seeing exactly where the data is located in relation to the note events.

42 Controlling and Interpreting MIDI Data: Answers and Commentary

Electric guitar: slide

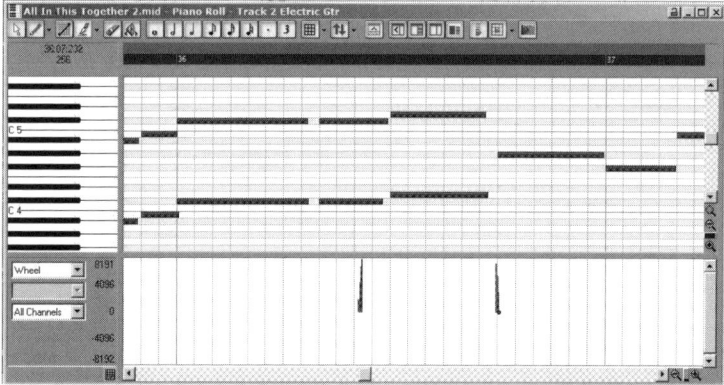

In Sonar, pitch bend is referred to as wheel in the drop down menu on the bottom left. In Cubase, it appears in the full list of MIDI controllers.

Bass: grace note

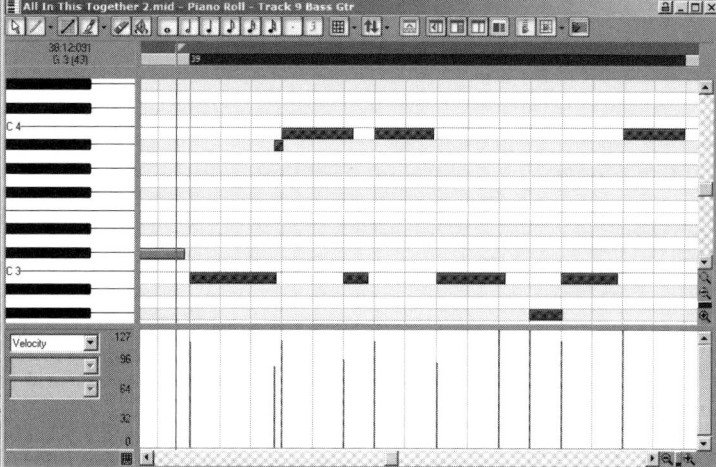

One method of creating grace notes would be to input two pitches, the first being quite short and completely legato, leaving no gap between the end of the first note and the start of the second. See the example above (bar 39).

The velocity is slightly lower for the grace note. This would be played in this editor, making sure the snap to grid is off or set to a low value so short notes can be created.

Controlling and Interpreting MIDI Data: Answers and Commentary 43

Lead guitar: hammer on

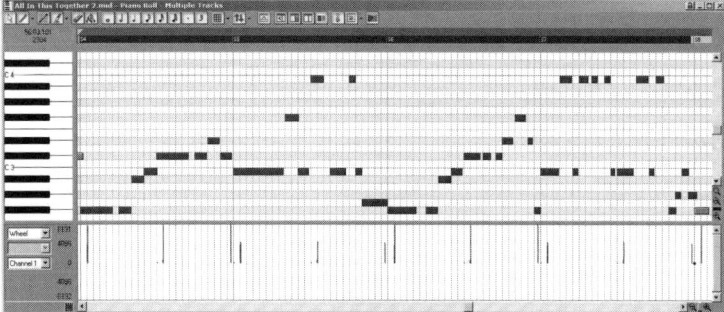

Note the way the almost instant change in pitch is achieved.

All tracks except electric guitar: fade at end

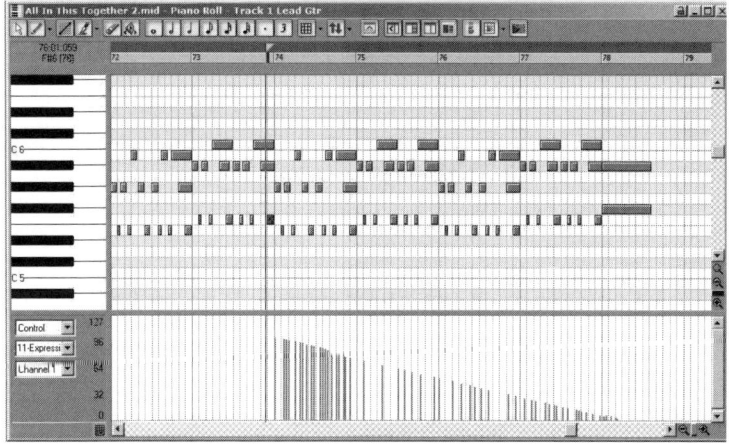

As with the hammond/volume, a smooth ramp would have been achieved using the line tool. There is often confusion about when to use Main Volume (controller 7) and Expression (controller 11) as they appear to have the same function. Expression should create changes in dynamics, acting within each track to make parts louder or quieter; it can also change the level during a note – tailing off the level of a long held note for example. Main Volume is best used for the overall level of tracks and balancing the levels of the instruments within the mix. Best use Main Volume at the beginning, that sets the relative level to give a clear mix, as an engineer would do with a multi-track recording. Variations within the performance are then handled using Expression. In this MIDI file, there is no variation in Main Volume, as discussed in question 10.

A final word

You will find more variety of sequencing techniques in your actual exam than presented here, where the principles of being a 'MIDI detective' are only outlined. You will have to extend that way of thinking to analysis of other sequencing techniques mentioned in the Key Terms and Concepts section of this guide.

A2 6718/02
Music Technology in Context

INTRODUCTION TO THE PAPER

When does it happen?

The Music Technology in Context paper [6718/02] takes place in June on the same morning that you sit the Unit 6 – Paper 1: Controlling and Interpreting MIDI Data paper [6718/01].

How long is it?

The examination lasts one hour.

How many questions are there?

You will be given either Paper 2A: Music for the Moving Image or Paper 2B: Words and Music, depending on which Area of Study you have followed. There are seven questions: everyone answers questions 1 to 5 and **you choose** to answer **either** question 6 **or** question 7.

How many marks can I achieve?

The paper is marked out of 50 then added to the marks achieved in Paper I. This combined mark makes up 40% of the total mark for A2.

Is there anything else I should know?

You will be given an audio CD with all the extracts you require to answer the questions. You will need something on which to play the CD (portable CD player, laptop/computer with CD drive and so on) and some good-quality headphones on which to listen to it. The CD will contain the complete track listing but you do not have to listen to every piece all the way through. Within the time limit you may listen to each track as many times as you wish.

ANSWERING THE QUESTIONS – WHAT THE BOARD WANTS

What is being assessed?

Candidates are expected to demonstrate 'their knowledge and understanding of a range of music related to Area of Study 4'. Candidates must either answer questions on **Music for the Moving Image** or **Words and Music**.

The questions fall into two categories:
- Those relating directly to the recorded extracts on the CD
- Those asking the candidates to demonstrate 'their understanding of historical, technological and contextual issues' related to their chosen Area of Study.

Presenting your answers

The questions relating to the recorded extracts on the CD require multiple choice, completion of grids, short sentences and bullet point-type answers, identifying features of tracks, labelling structural sections, naming techniques, often worth one mark each.

The questions that ask the candidate to demonstrate 'their understanding of historical, technological and contextual issues' related to their chosen Area of Study require continuous prose, amounting to a short essay. You should **not** answer these questions with short notes, lists or bullet points.

Marks per question

It is important to look at the number of marks available for each question. If there is a grid to be completed with eight spaces it is fair to assume that each correctly completed item will score one mark. The questions that require longer answers will have eight or ten marks available; this means that **at least** eight or ten relevant points need to be made in order to score maximum marks.

Don't waffle

Stick to what is being asked; don't drift off into information that is not being asked for. Think carefully about the question and make sure everything you write is relevant to it. Anything that is irrelevant, however interesting, will be ignored by the examiner, will receive no marks and wastes valuable time.

HOW TO APPROACH REVISION

Organising your time

The secret is to do a little revision, but do it often. Don't attempt to revise an entire film or album in one sitting: one song, or two or three film cues per revision session will give effective results. Read your notes, listen to the track(s) and make sure that you can answer the questions suggested in the relevant sections of this book. If you can't answer some questions make sure you revisit those tracks in the following few days.

Practising questions

Although this paper has now been set for some years, these particular set works are new for 2008, so there are no questions available from past papers directly relating to the current set works. However, the questions that have been set about earlier set works can easily be applied, or adjusted, to the works on the current specification.

Revision tips

- Link your notes to your listening: read your notes on a track, listen to the track, then read your notes again
- Write out the features of a track and tick them off as you hear them; if you don't spot something listen again until you do
- Listen and make notes; jot down what you are hearing
- Listen, don't just hear; listening requires you to actively concentrate whereas hearing is a passive activity which does not require your brain to be engaged
- Never revise with distractions, particularly other noises such as television or radio; work in a quiet room away from anything which might prevent you from focusing on the task at hand
- Try to listen using the same headphones that you will use in the exam to get used to how they feel and check out their quality; if possible use the same CD playback device in order to get used to the controls.

THE AREAS OF STUDY

There are two Areas of Study, each with its own set works to study:

Music for the Moving Image

Covers two film soundtracks:
- *Goldfinger*
- *Batman*

Words and Music

Covers two albums:
- *Who's Next:* The Who
- *The Immaculate Collection:* Madonna

You will have studied **one** of these two Areas of Study and you will receive a paper that has questions relating only to that particular Area of Study. The next two chapters will focus on these two Areas of Study.

Area of Study 6718/02A
Music for the Moving Image

This Area of Study is about music for film and television. You need to be familiar with the two core films: *Goldfinger* and *Batman*.

A brief history of film music

The earliest films (Lumière brothers, 1895) used live music performed by a pianist or small band to cover the sound of noisy projectors. Silent movies continued to use pianists, pit bands and even orchestras in films such as *Birth of a Nation* (1915). *The Jazz Singer* (1927) was one of the first successful sound films and led to the demise of live music for film, although it led to the advent of composers providing recorded film scores.

Max Steiner was probably the first specialist film composer. Notable scores by Steiner include *King Kong* (1933), *Gone with the Wind* (1939) and *Casablanca* (1942). Bernard Hermann composed film scores that gave a psychological insight into the characters in films such as Orson Welles' *Citizen Kane* (1941), and Alfred Hitchcock's *North by Northwest* (1959) and *Psycho* (1960).

Popular music was increasingly used in films following the inclusion of *Do Not Forsake Me Oh My Darlin'* in the western *High Noon* (1952). Other films which have used pop songs effectively include *Breakfast at Tiffany's* (1961), *Robin Hood: Prince of Thieves* (1991) and the James Bond series of films.

Large orchestral scores came back into fashion in the 1970s thanks, in some part, to the collaboration between director Steven Spielberg and composer John Williams on films such as *Jaws* (1975), *Raiders of the Lost Ark* (1981), *Jurassic Park* (1993) and *Saving Private Ryan* (1998), as well as his scores for the *Star Wars* series of films.

The roles of film music

Film music has a number of functions:

1. **Title music**, either opening or ending, to set up the mood at the beginning of the film or to bring the film to a conclusion while the credit sequence rolls.
2. **Underscoring**, sometimes called background music, supports the on-screen action and, often, enhances it with techniques such as the use of leitmotif (see overleaf) – recollecting earlier events or hinting at events still to come.
3. **Pastiche** can be used to reflect a bygone age or historical period, such as much of Dario Marianelli's score for *Pride and Prejudice* (2005)
4. **Evocative music** can suggest a place or a setting, such as John Williams' use of Jewish musical characteristics in his score for *Schindler's List* (1993) or the Austrian zither to suggest Vienna in *The Third Man* (1949).

5. **Mickey Mousing** is music that directly mimics the on-screen action, such as a character creeping up behind someone else with each step being accompanied by a chord.
6. **Illustrative music**, while depicting the on-screen action, is not a musical mimicry in the way that mickey mousing is. Both William Walton (1944) and Patrick Doyle (1989) wrote musical illustrations of the Battle of Agincourt in two different film versions of Shakespeare's *Henry V*.
7. **Dramatic music** enhances the on-screen drama in ways such as making romantic moments seem more romantic or scary moments seem more scary.
8. **Leitmotifs** are recurring musical themes, chord sequences or rhythms linked to represent a particular person, place or idea. In classical music, Wagner used leitmotifs in his *The Ring of the Nibelung* cycle of four operas. In film music, leitmotifs are common. Below are some examples:
   - Howard Shore's scores for *The Lord of the Rings* films use many leitmotifs to represent characters and places
   - John Williams' *Star Wars* scores include the *Imperial March* linked to appearances by Darth Vader, and leitmotifs for Luke Skywalker, Princess Leia, Yoda and Emperor Palpatine
   - Max Steiner's score for *Gone with the Wind* uses many leitmotifs including Tara's theme representing the O'Hara house in Georgia.
9. **Diegetic music**, also known as featured music, is music which is part of the on-screen action, that characters actually hear, such as music on the television, an ensemble performing at a ball or a band marching by. Good examples are the opening dance number in *Indiana Jones and the Temple of Doom* (1984) or Michael J Fox playing *Johnny B Goode* on electric guitar in *Back to the Future* (1985).

Things you must know for Music for the Moving Image

Make sure that you can answer the following questions about **each film**:
- In which year was the film released?
- Who directed and produced the film? What other films have they worked on (particularly earlier films that may have influenced this film)?
- Who composed the soundtrack? What other films have they worked on (particularly earlier films that may have influenced this film)?
- What is the genre of the film? (Western, sci-fi, romance and so on.)
- What is the basic plot?
- What is the style of music? Is this consistent throughout the film? What other musical styles influence this score?
- What instrumentation does the composer use? Does this stay the same throughout the film? Are there any unusual instruments/sound sources?
- What roles does the music take in the film?

Make sure you can answer the following questions about **each musical cue**:
- At what point does the music start? What is happening at that point?
- Is the entry a subtle fade-in, a sudden loud entry or something else? Does it synchronise with a specific on-screen action or event?
- What mood is the composer trying to create and how is this achieved? Refer to melody, harmony, texture, timbre and structure.
- How does this cue relate to other cues either earlier or later in the film? Does it use similar material? Is the music altered/developed in any way?

GOLDFINGER: JOHN BARRY (1964)

Remember that this book is a revision guide. For a more in-depth analysis, refer to *John Barry's Goldfinger in Focus* written by Barry Russell (Rhinegold Publishing, 2007: ISBN 978-1-906178-10-9).

Background info

Director: Guy Hamilton, whose other films include *Funeral in Berlin* (1966), *Battle of Britain* (1969), *Force 10 from Navarone* (1978) and *Evil Under the Sun* (1982). Also the following James Bond movies: *Diamonds are Forever* (1971), *Live and Let Die* (1973) and *The Man with the Golden Gun* (1975).

Plot: While James Bond is investigating Auric Goldfinger (a gold dealer whom the Bank of England suspects is stockpiling large amounts of gold bullion), he uncovers a sinister plot called Operation Grand Slam (to raid Fort Knox and detonate an atomic device in the vault). Bond races against time to foil Goldfinger's plans and overthrows the plot just in time.

Composer: John Barry has written the music for several other James Bond movies: *Dr No* (1962), *From Russia with Love* (1963), *Thunderball* (1965), *You Only Live Twice* (1967), *On Her Majesty's Secret Service* (1969), *Diamonds are Forever* (1971), *The Man with the Golden Gun* (1974), *Moonraker* (1979), *Octopussy* (1983), *A View to a Kill* (1985) and *The Living Daylights* (1987). Other non-James Bond film scores include *The Lion in Winter* (1968), *Jagged Edge* (1985), *Out of Africa* (1985) and *Dances with Wolves* (1990).

Score: Orchestra with the following parts:
- Strings – first and second violins, violas, cellos, double bass and harp
- Woodwind – flute (plus piccolo), oboe (plus cor anglais) and tenor saxophone
- Brass – four horns, four trumpets, three trombones (two tenor, one bass) and tuba
- Percussion.

Possible focus of questions
- Relationship between on-screen action and the music
- Compositional devices
- Use of leitmotifs.

Leitmotifs

Goldfinger is represented by three leitmotifs all developed from the title song 'Goldfinger':
- 'Gold 1' – a pair of chords (F major and D♭ major)
- 'Gold 2' – a three-note motif with an ascending perfect 5th and a descending major 2nd (used for the word 'Goldfinger' in the title song)
- 'Gold 3' – a falling major 3rd and an ascending major 2nd (used for the words 'He's the man' in the title song)

James Bond is represented by two musical ideas taken from Monty Norman's *James Bond Theme*, originally heard in the first James Bond movie *Dr No* (1962):
- 'Bond 1' – an off-beat pedal note (A) over which the interval of a perfect 5th rises two semitones before falling a semitone in minims (E – F♮ – F♯ – F♮)
- 'Bond 2' – the well-known *James Bond Theme* which uses 'Bond 1' as an accompaniment (in a two-bar ostinato)

Other leitmotifs include:
- 'Menace' motif – a rhythm made up of three triplet crotchets followed by two straight crotchets, played on timpani and snare drum
- 'Auric 1' – a four-note idea (C – B♭ – E♭ – C) representing Goldfinger's organisation
- 'Spy chord' – the chord of E minor with a major 9th, first heard in 'Bond Back In Action Again'
- 'Three Blind Mice' – three descending notes (E♭ – D – C) used throughout the film to represent failure.

Cues

The cues are in the order they appear in the film rather than the order on the soundtrack CD.

Bond Back In Action Again
- Stabbing 'Spy chords', 'Bond 1' and 'Bond 2' immediately set up a mood of excitement with an undertone of something a little ominous
- Slower **tempo** with **muted** trombones and marimba
- 'Bond 1' scored in extremes – very high violins with off-beat double basses
- 'Gold 2' is heard on saxophone and then horns
- Marimba plays a 'ticking' **ostinato** combined with **muted** brass
- 'Three Blind Mice' idea is introduced by **muted** brass
- Cue ends on high violins.

Main title – *Goldfinger*

- Sung by Shirley Bassey
- Song – opens with 'Gold 1' and 'Gold 2' combined, starts loud but **diminuendo** and reduced scoring lead over to the vocal part
- Vocal accompanied by lush strings
- String fills rather than drum fills
- Adventurous **harmony** – for example, chord changes from A major to E♭ major (a diminished 5th away)
- 'Bond 1' is heard in the **middle 8** played by brass
- Much use of **triplets**.

Into Miami

- Two-chord pattern – A♭ minor to D♭7
- Harp **glissandi**
- Saxophone melody accompanied by a new two-chord progression (A♭ minor – B♭ minor 6)
- Jazz harmonies resolve to a chord of A♭ major.

Golden Girl

- 'Gold 1', performed by low brass, has a chord of C minor with a major 7th added – plus hints of 'Bond 1' in timpani and pizzicato strings
- Music suggests a funeral with regular slow beat
- **Flutter-tongued** flute descending **semitone** idea is accompanied by crotales, harp and xylophone
- 'Auric 1' is heard on brass before cue ends on F minor chord played by strings and harp.

Alpine Drive

- 'Gold 1' and 'Gold 2' are heard
- Trumpets using **Harmon mutes** play stabs on the note C while timpani play an idea on a tritone (C – F♯)
- Instrumental version of 'Main Title' with lush orchestration and violins playing melody. When they go up an **octave** there are harp **glissandi** and sustained brass
- 'Bond 1' in A minor – **middle 8** melody performed by horns – **double-time** feel created by ride cymbal with brushes and **walking bass**
- Violins play **smears** – short **glissandi**
- Original **tempo** – flute **trills**
- Sudden interruption of string **tremolando** (performed fp).

Auric's Factory

- Horns introduce 'Auric 1' over a low **pedal** in basses
- Use of **rubato** – short **rallentandos** and **accelerandos**
- Faster **tempo** – irregular stabbing **dyads** (two-note chords) on muted brass against a high **pedal** on high strings (**tremolando**)
- Timpani play 'Auric 1'
- Return to F minor, slower **tempo**, harp and vibraphone (played with motor on to create a throbbing/wah effect)
- Harp **ostinato** is the second and third notes of 'Gold 2'
- Cue ends with stabbing 'Spy Chord'.

Death of Tilly

- This cue is a variation of 'Golden Girl' to show that Tilly is Jill's sister
- 'Gold 1' – C minor, snare drum with punchy chords
- Violin **anacrusis** leads to low harp, plays C minor triad followed by G minor triad under a **pedal** G
- Cello **anacrusis** leads to a sad **descending** idea
- Timpani leads to a low brass chord of C minor
- Harp **ostinato** (based around C minor with added 6th and 9th) accompanies repeat of sad idea – violin **pedal** G throughout
- Harp ostinato and violin pedal continues; muted trumpets and flute play two-note interruptions irregularly
- Plaintive melody played by flute and oboe.

The Laser Beam

- Cue is based on **ostinato** patterns and building textures
- Opening **ostinato** using the 'Menace' leitmotif
- 'Gold 2' is added over the **ostinato**
- New **ostinato** figure played by violins – listen for the **glissandi**
- High pedal F and brass thicken and extend the texture
- Low brass are added – all gets thicker and louder to increase tension
- Cue ends with an F minor chord for **divisi** solo strings.

Pussy Galore's Flying Circus

- Carousel-like **ostinato** (**riff**) and a $\frac{12}{8}$ feel with 'Gold 2' on horns
- Mood change – darker – C minor
- **Tempo** increases a little and harmony moves between F major and C minor
- 'Gold 2' played on **tremolando** strings
- Crotales play descending **semitone** figure heard previously in 'Golden Girl'
- Trombones play 'Gold 1'

- $\frac{12}{8}$ returns, harp **glissandi**
- 'Gold 1' and 'Gold 2' with saxophone
- Strings play 'Goldfinger' theme and a trumpet, with Harmon mute tube extended, adds a wah effect.

Teasing the Korean

- Low F minor chord played on strings – 'Auric' played on low harp
- Saxophone plays a jazzy version of 'Gold 2' combined with 'Auric'
- Horns, trumpets and piccolo play a new version of 'Gold 2' which is combined with the second and third notes of 'Gold 2'
- Cor anglais repeats melody played earlier in cue by saxophone
- 'Menace' motif is heard on brass, snare drum and timpani over an F minor chord
- A new version of 'Gold 2' is played by harp
- The cue ends with the 'Menace' motif on **pizzicato** cellos and double basses with timpani.

Gassing the Gangsters

- 'Gold 1' on low brass – timpani and **pizzicato** double basses
- Trumpets play in their low register
- High crotale and xylophone
- 'Menace' motif followed by 'screaming' idea on piccolo, flute and muted trumpet leads to 'Gold 2' over an F major chord.

Oddjob's Pressing Engagement

- Brass and strings play a chord of C7 but with a **flattened** fifth producing a **tritone**
- Single note from harp leads to 'kiss of death' from main title song which, in turn, leads to 'Bond 1' with offbeat trombones
- The **middle 8** from the main title song leads, via 'Auric 1' to 'Gold 1' with an impressive timpani part
- 'Gold 2' – then modulates to 'Bond 1' combined with 'Gold 2' to depict the conflict
- Opening chord returns but with a pedal G♭ to emphasise the **tritone** – harp outlines the chord, brass play the chord like a pulse, flute **flutter-tonguing**
- 'Gold 1' with prominent timpani, 'Gold 2' on trumpets, then modulates through to 'Bond 1' and 'Gold 2' then 'He loves only gold' from the **coda** (**outro**) of the song
- Slower **tempo**, brass **flutter-tongue** 'Gold 2'
- Oboe and saxophone introduce new idea in F minor – brass and timpani add a pulsing F minor chord
- The 'Menace' motif leads to the oboe and saxophone bringing the cue to a quiet end.

Dawn Raid on Fort Knox

- A long cue created through building **ostinato** patterns
- 'Gold 1' plus snare drum providing a militaristic feeling
- Flute, oboe and violins play a long held C on which they **crescendo** and **diminuendo**
- 'Gold 2' on trumpets with adapted ending
- Violins introduce a running **semiquaver** idea which continues as a layer in the texture; 'Gold 2' on trumpets – new brass idea
- Unexpected interruption of the 'Menace' motif on low brass, snare drum and timpani on D♭7 chord (also unexpected)
- Violin running **semiquavers** return – 'Menace' – new brass idea (as before) – high-pitched version of 'Gold 2'
- **Staccato** xylophone represents gunshots
- Horns play 'Gold 2' – staccato xylophone – violin running **semiquavers**
- Falling minor 2nd on piccolo and violins – horns answer with variation of 'Gold 2' – staccato xylophone returns a **semitone** higher than before
- Insistent timpani accompany falling minor 2nd on piccolo and violins – 'Menace' motif – triumphant percussion
- 'Menace' motif is adapted to show that the operation is being successful; 'Spy chord' played by strings – timpani roll
- Trumpets play the new brass idea from earlier – 'Gold 2' is played high-pitched – staccato xylophone returns
- 'Menace' motif dies down into the 'Spy chord'
- Low strings and timpani pound out a note which is sometimes on the beat and sometimes **syncopated**
- Music resolves on to a held C.

The Arrival of the Bomb and Countdown

- Much slower than previous cue to increase tension
- Fragments from the militaristic timpani and snare drum punctuate repeated C minor chords
- 'Gold 3' played by low muted trumpets; falling **semitone** 'Golden Girl'
- Xylophone and violins lead to a pause – **time signature** changes to $^6_8$ (from $^4_4$) – F minor chord with added 7th and 9th followed by F minor with a diminished 5th (the **tritone**)
- March idea returns – falling minor 2nd on brass – 'Menace' motif returns – xylophone repeated G leads to C minor
- Low brass play a variation of 'Gold 2' with **blue-note** decoration
- Violins play falling minor 2nd answered by upward **glissando** on harp
- 'Gold 2' – C minor with added major 7th – high glockenspiel – cue ends on a **tritone**.

The Death of Goldfinger (End Titles)

- Block orchestrations contrast flute, trumpets and high strings with low brass, snare drum and timpani – repeated with 'Auric' motif on low brass and the 'Menace' motif on snare drum:
- High string **triplets**
- 'Gold 2' on horns and very high trumpets (screaming)
- Harp **glissandi** – 'Menace' motif
- 'Gold 2' played very high by violins coincides with Goldfinger's death
- End titles are an instrumental version of the main title song – horns take on the vocal line and the piece is re-orchestrated to sound very lush and sensuous.

Goldfinger – Instrumental

- This track is on the soundtrack album but not heard in the film – it is therefore very unlikely to have questions set about it
- It is not merely a re-orchestration of the song but a reworking with musical ideas from the 'Dawn Raid On Fort Knox' used and the melody played by guitar (the main melody instrument in the 'James Bond Theme').

BATMAN – DANNY ELFMAN (1989)

Remember that this book is a revision guide. For a more in-depth analysis, refer to *Danny Elfman's Batman in Focus* written by Mark Wilderspin (Rhinegold Publishing, 2007: ISBN 978-1-906178-09-3).

Background info

Director: Tim Burton – other films include *Beetlejuice* (1988), *Mars Attacks!* (1996), *Planet of the Apes* (2001) and *Charlie and the Chocolate Factory* (2005)

Plot: A young boy who witnesses his parents' murder on the streets of Gotham City grows up to become the Batman – a mysterious crime-fighting hero. He emerges from the shadows when the Joker appears – a horribly disfigured individual out to seek revenge on his former employer.

Composer: Danny Elfman has worked on many projects with director Tim Burton, including *Charlie and the Chocolate Factory* (2005) but has also written scores for films such as *Spider-Man* (2002) and *Charlotte's Web* (2006). He has also written television themes such as *The Simpsons* and *Desperate Housewives*.

Score: Large orchestra with synthesisers and voices.

Remember that there are two soundtrack albums for *Batman*: one containing songs by Prince (The Motion Picture Soundtrack) and one with a selection of Danny Elfman's music from the original score (The Motion Picture Score) – you are being examined on your knowledge of Danny Elfman's score.

Possible focus of questions

- Relationship between on-screen action and the music
- Development of leitmotif, musical structures and compositional techniques
- Recognition of instruments and instrumental techniques.

Cues

Batman Theme

- Opens with the five-note motif (B – C♯ – D – G – F♯) that acts as Batman's **leitmotif** throughout the film, played slowly, then **layered** on top of itself in different **rhythms**
- The five-note **motif** is extended to six notes as the music builds to a triumphant chord of C♯ major – this unexpected chord coincides with the presentation of the title 'Batman' on screen
- **Tempo** picks up – **march-style** – five-note **motif** is now **triplet quavers** followed by two **crotchets**
- The whole cue is made up of similar **repetitions**, **developments** and **extensions** of the 'Batman Theme' (often resulting in unexpected modulations).

Roof Fight

- Layered **ostinati**, pounding percussion, rapidly running string parts and use of the Batman theme make up most of this short cue.

Shootout/First Confrontation

- Rocking **ostinato** with $\frac{6}{8}$ feel (**time signature** is $\frac{3}{4}$) in cellos, violas and low piano
- Use of **tritone** interval – **diminished 5th** between each half of the $\frac{6}{8}$ bar
- Additional **ostinato** layers include:
    a Violins and trumpets playing a four-**semiquaver** figure followed by quaver figure
    b Trumpets playing six repeated **semiquavers**, answered by trombones an **octave** lower
    c A pair of **semiquavers** on each **crotchet** beat (producing a **cross-rhythm** effect of $\frac{3}{4}$ and $\frac{6}{8}$ together
- Use of **whole-tone scale** in third section of cue to show uncertainty combined with sparse textures and less movement than the rest of the cue.

Kitchen, Surgery, Face Off

- A gentle and contemplative start featuring strings, harp and horn
- Interjections from **atonal** piano, bassoon and low strings lead to sustained notes and a piano **trill** which builds up
- A brash circus-like **waltz** for full orchestra dies away to just a celesta.

Flowers
- In $\frac{3}{4}$, with a melody reminiscent of the Batman-theme – gentle
- A brief interlude of forceful string chords.

Clown Attack
- Low piano and **pizzicato** strings; hints of Herrmann's score for *Psycho* (1960)
- Lots of interplay between parts, echo, question and answer
- Layered texture dominated by strings – limited percussion (just a snare drum).

Batman to the Rescue
- Similar bass ostinato to previous cue opens this cue
- Big orchestra – with outbursts from brass and percussion
- Use of Batman-theme with lots of percussion, notably cymbals – then tom-toms combined with low piano
- Orchestral **stabs**
- Repeated xylophone figure then gradually more layered percussion ostinati
- Pounding bass figure – triplet quavers, crotchet
- Brass **flutter-tongues** and timpani solo – cheeky ending.

Roasted Dude
- Layers of vibraphone, guiro, and orchestral effects including trombone **glissandi**.

Photos/Beautiful Dreamer
- Simple piano and **sustained** strings accompany woodwind melody
- Sinister **waltz** using musical saw portamento
- Interpolated music: Stephen Foster's *Beautiful Dreamer* on harp and celesta before lush string arrangement with an abrupt ending.

Descent into Mystery
- Running string semiquavers to give urgency, pounding low piano, vocal parts – layered **ostinati** – very ominous
- Batman-theme with tubular bells
- Triumphant ending in **major key**.

The Bat Cave
- Magical sounds – harp, solo violin
- Sustained chords – use of string **tremolando** – over a relentless bass ostinato.

The Joker's Poem

- Glockenspiels, solo violin, lush strings – a sense of the grotesque
- Abrupt, loud ending recalling the Joker's waltz.

Childhood Remembered

- Also known as 'Challenge/Dream'
- Most of cue accompanies a flashback as Bruce Wayne realises that the Joker (in his previous incarnation as Jack Napier) murdered his parents
- Entire cue in A minor with a tonic pedal throughout – given pace by pulsating piano and bass drum beat
- **Collage** textures, use of downward **pitch-bend**, processed vocal sounds.

Love Theme

- Based on the Batman-theme – the second note is **flattened** (B – C – D – G – F♯) and it is now **harmonised** in G major.

Charge of the Batmobile

- Slow **introduction** based on the Batman-theme, rhythmically indistinct
- Faster section, based on the Batman-theme **modulating** through many **keys**
- **Coda** uses material from 'Descent Into Mystery' but a louder orchestration.

Attack of the Batwing

- Builds up – **martial** drumming, Batman-theme, **syncopation**, brass **trills**
- Tubular bells and timpani prominent
- Layered **ostinati**
- Abrupt **modulations** at end of Batman-theme
- Repeated notes with **accented** notes to give a sense of unease
- The pounding triplet figure from earlier returns
- Descending **arpeggio** figures on piano.

Up the Cathedral

- Tremolando strings
- Church organ to symbolise the cathedral
- Batman-theme with abrupt **modulations**
- Shrill flute and piccolo **trills** combined with organ
- Much use of layered **ostinati**.

Waltz (to the Death)

- In **rondo form** (Intro – A – A – B – A – C – A – D – A – End)
- Generally the music gets higher in pitch and faster to add tension
- The Joker appears to actually dance to the music.

The Final Confrontation

- Long organ chords beneath orchestra
- Use of **flutter-tonguing**
- Layered **ostinati**, percussion outbursts, harp **glissandi**, extreme dynamics, prominent snare drum, hints at Batman-theme, gong
- Running **semiquavers** – juxtaposition of ideas, some quiet, some loud
- Recaps of Batman-theme played softly and Joker's waltz.

Finale

- Triumphant version of Batman-theme – generally more **major** (but still with abrupt **modulations**) – recap of 'Love Theme' – big brass finale with bells and timpani.

Batman Theme Reprise

- A reworked and shorter version of the opening.

PUTTING BOTH FILMS INTO CONTEXT

In order to put both films into context it is important that you have some knowledge of, and have listened to and watched, some other spy and crime-fighting movies.

Here are some suggestions:

- Anton Karas' score for *The Third Man* (1949) with its distinctive use of zither
- Ennio Morricone's score for *The Untouchables* (1987)
- Howard Shore's score for *Seven* (1995)
- Jerry Goldsmith's score for *L.A. Confidential* (1997).

Area of Study 6718/02B
Words and Music

This Area of Study is about the relationship of words and music in popular song.

You need to be familiar with the two core albums: *Who's Next* – The Who; *The Immaculate Collection* – Madonna.

Things you must know for Words and Music

Make sure that you can answer the following questions about **each album**:
- In what year was the album released?
- What is the musical style of the album? Is it consistent?
- Other than the performers, did anyone else write any of the songs?
- What other albums have the performers released? How does this album fit within these?

Make sure you can answer the following questions about **each song**:
- What is the structure of the song?
- What is the range of the melody?
- How does the music reflect the words? Are there any specific points about word-setting?
- Is there any melismatic treatment of the lyrics?
- Are the phrases regular?
- Is the key major or minor? Does this stay consistent through the song?
- Is the choice of harmony simple or complex? Does this help to enhance the lyrics?
- Are there any unusual chords? What is their purpose?
- What is the instrumentation of the song?
- What special effects have been used? Why?

WHO'S NEXT: THE WHO (1971)

Remember that this book is a revision guide. For a more in-depth analysis, refer to *The Who: Who's Next* written by Julien Winterson (Rhinegold Publishing, 2007: ISBN 978-1-906178-12-3).

Background Info

Group: The Who is an English rock band, formed in 1964. Initially the members were Roger Daltrey (vocals), Pete Townshend (guitar), John Entwistle (bass) and Keith Moon (drums). Keith Moon died in 1978 from a drug overdose. They were renowned for their live shows, in which they often destroyed their instruments. The Who has released 12 albums, some of which had a theatrical slant including *Tommy* (1969) and *Quadrophenia* (1973), which are considered to be rock-operas.

Album: Released in 1971, it was The Who's sixth album and is widely considered to be the band's greatest album, appearing on several 'Top 100' and 'Greatest Album' lists. The album was originally intended to be a follow-up to *Tommy*, called the *Lifehouse Project*, but instead is a series of nine unrelated tracks with no narrative linking them. The album produced two singles; *Behind Blue Eyes* and *Won't Get Fooled Again* (both released in 1971). Remastered and deluxe editions of the album include extra and bonus tracks.

Possible focus of questions

- Relationship between lyrics and music
- Compositional devices and structure
- Use of technology.

Tracks

Baba O'Riley

- Often mistakenly called *Teenage Wasteland* because of the chorus lyrics, the title refers to Meher Baba (the Indian spiritual teacher who claimed to be an avatar) and Terry Riley (the pioneering American **minimalist** composer)
- $\frac{4}{4}$ time signature and largely based on three chords: F, C and B♭ (chords I, V and IV in the key of F major) this song has a **prog rock** feel
- Structure: Intro, Verse 1, Bridge, Verse 2, Guitar solo, Chorus, Coda
- Opens with repetitive pattern reminiscent of a **tape loop** (but, unlike a loop, this does change through the song)
- The vocals are shared between Townshend and Daltrey – listen carefully for the different vocal **timbres**
- The chorus has an ABAB structure and, at the end of the chorus, the **tempo** changes leading into the **coda** that includes a violin solo and a **modal**/Eastern feel. The music gets faster and becomes klezmer-like with frenetic drumming building to a **plagal cadence** (chord IV – chord I).

Bargain

- Structure: Intro, Verse 1, Verse 2, Chorus, Verse 3, Verse 4, Chorus, Middle Eight, Verse 5, Verse 6, Chorus, Coda
- $\frac{4}{4}$ **time-signature**; key of B♭ major but with added **blue notes** (flattened 3rd, 5th and 7th)
- There is debate as to whether the 'you' in the lyrics is part of a general love song or whether it is Meher Baba
- Intro uses synthesiser (sounding like a reversed tape) and acoustic guitar **strummed**
- Daltrey sing the verses, Townshend joins in the middle-eight section
- Middle eight has change of **texture** and **dynamics**, the **overdriven guitar** drops out and the kick drum and snare drum are brought forward in the mix
- The coda is played by the synthesiser.

Love Ain't for Keepin'

- A short song (just over two minutes) that has two acoustic guitar parts (one **strummed**, one **picked**) and a complicated descending **semiquaver** bass guitar **riff**
- Written in the **mixolydian mode** (the major scale with a **flattened 7th** or the white notes on a piano from G to G)
- Mostly 4/4 but changes to 2/4 when the title lyrics are sung
- Structure: Intro, Verse 1, Verse 2, Coda (with the last line of the verse repeated three times)
- At 'Lay down beside me' the **dynamics** get softer
- At 'Love Ain't for Keepin'' the **dynamics** get louder
- Unusual ending – sustained chord seems to be end but there is a final guitar flourish.

My Wife

- Written by John Entwistle, who also takes on the role of lead vocals, this is a jokey song about a frightened husband and the lyrics are deliberately overstated
- Entwistle's vocals have been **double tracked** to thicken the sound of the voice, with each track panned hard left and hard right (modern recording techniques would put both double tracked vocals at the same position in the stereo field)
- Has long sustained notes on the **flugelhorn** (brass instrument associated with brass bands and jazz) and trumpet **stabs**
- End of song repeats the words 'She's coming', gradually fading.

The Song is Over

- Originally intended as the final song of the *Lifehouse Project*
- Structure: Intro, Verse 1, Verse 2, Chorus, Middle Eight, Verse 3, Instrumental, Verse 4, Coda
- A ballad – begins in B♭ major but ends in C major having gone through several **modulations**
- Begins with gentle piano playing **broken chords** with a synthesiser backing
- Drums don't enter until the second verse
- In the second verse, the third line is raised a **tone** making it a **sequence** of the first line – also the seventh line is a **sequence** of the fifth line
- The fourth verse has an extended final line reflecting the lyrics 'Even if it takes a million years' that leads to a quotation from another Who song, *Pure and Easy*.

Getting in Tune

- Structure: Intro, Verse 1, Verse 2, Chorus, Verse 3, Coda
- A love song – 'Getting in tune' being used with two meanings – the musical act of being in tune together and emotionally being in tune with a partner
- Begins with quiet piano chords
- The verses have the structure: A – A – B – C – D

- The chorus has **call and response** between soloist and backing vocals
- Verse 3 is softer to build tension before the ending that includes the musicians **improvising**.

Going Mobile
- Structure: Verse 1, Verse 2, Middle Eight, Verse 3, Final section
- A happy song in a major **key**
- Middle eight adds a synthesiser and changes the **rhythm** and **dynamics** – it also has a new **chord sequence**
- Final section includes a solo performed on **improvised** guitar synthesiser over busy band **accompaniment**.

Behind Blue Eyes
- An enigmatic song with lyrics whose meaning even members of the band disagree about
- Begins quietly with acoustic guitar **picking** a **broken chord** of E minor
- Second verse has additional vocal **harmonies** and a louder **dynamic** – towards the end of the verse the acoustic guitar changes to a **syncopated strummed** pattern.

Won't Get Fooled Again
- A long song – just under nine minutes – containing many characteristics of **prog rock**. It is an anti-war **protest song** (the main focus of political protest at the time was the Vietnam War)
- Structure: Intro, Verse 1, Chorus, Middle Eight, Verse 2, Chorus, Middle Eight, Instrumental, Verse 3, Chorus, Synth solo, Coda
- Begins with **psychedelic** synthesiser chords (an effect produced through **filtering**)
- Guitar uses **power chords**
- Song is largely based on three chords
- Synthesiser plays throughout and has a moment of glory with a solo towards the end.

THE IMMACULATE COLLECTION: MADONNA (1990)

Remember that this book is a revision guide. For a more in-depth analysis, refer to *Madonna: The Immaculate Collection* written by Adrian York (Rhinegold Publishing, 2007: ISBN 978-1-906178-11-6).

Background info

Singer: Madonna is one of the most innovative and influential musicians of the past quarter of a century and has rarely been far from the charts in the United States, the United Kingdom and across the globe. Born in Michigan in 1958, Madonna grew up in Detroit, the city famous for the Motown record label. She has always combined her music career with an acting career, although, in the early days, this was mostly as a vehicle for her recordings.

Album: Released in 1990 on the Sire record label, this was a 'Greatest Hits' album covering the first seven years of Madonna's recording career. It has 15 songs from six different albums and contains eight US number ones and six UK number ones (*Justify My Love* and *Rescue Me* were new songs on this album). The title is a play on the Roman Catholic dogma of the immaculate conception, deliberately chosen to echo her own name and to court controversy and maximise publicity. When the album was released it received some criticism because some of the earlier songs were remixes by Shep Pettibone and not the original single versions.

Possible focus of questions

- Relationship between lyrics and music
- Compositional devices and structure
- Use of technology.

Tracks

Holiday

- $\frac{4}{4}$, D major, 118 bpm
- Structure: Intro, 'Holiday' chant 1, Chorus, Verse 1, Bridge, Chorus, Instrumental Breakdown, Verse 2, Bridge, Chorus, Instrumental Breakdown, 'Holiday' chant, Chorus, 'Holiday' chant (fade)
- Busy Latin percussion including cowbell and bongos combined with classic disco four-to-the-floor style
- Chorus is **syllabic** and **diatonic**
- Verse and bridge use **pentatonic** melodies
- **Double-tracking** on 'We need a holiday' gives emphasis to the words
- The second 'Holiday' chant has only drums and percussion as an accompaniment.

Lucky Star

- $\frac{4}{4}$, E minor, 118 bpm
- Structure: Intro, Verse 1, Chorus, Verse 2, Chorus, Middle Eight, Verse 3, Chorus, Middle Eight, Verse 4, Chorus (with fade out)
- **Arpeggiated** synthesiser intro
- Verse and chorus use same three chords: E minor, C major, D major and two-bar **groove**
- Middle eight uses a **distorted guitar** and synthesised marimba
- Vocal in higher **register** except Verse 3 which uses a lower **register** – voice has a limited **compass** (most notes are within a 5th)
- Some words are half spoken to give emphasis.

Borderline

- $\frac{4}{4}$, D major, 119 bpm
- Structure: Intro (synthesiser followed by rhythm section), Verse 1, Bridge, Chorus, Rhythm Section Intro, Verse 2, Bridge, Chorus, Chorus (with fade out)

- Intro is in two-sections – synthesiser then rhythm section – after the first chorus the rhythm section intro is repeated
- Two-bar, three-chord **groove** – (D, C, G/B) for verse
- Bridge has **gospel-style** answering phrases
- Chorus begins a minor 3rd lower than Bridge and on a **first inversion** of the **dominant** chord rather than the **tonic**
- Vocal uses wide **compass**.

Like A Virgin

- 4/4, G♭ major, 119 bpm
- Structure: Intro, Verse 1, Bridge, Chorus, Verse 2, Bridge, Chorus, Middle Eight, Bridge, Chorus, Chorus, Chorus (with fade out)
- Synth bass and synthesiser chords, with hi-hat and kick drum, begin this song
- Almost child-like vocal delivery emphasising message of lyrics through Verse – note the synthesised harpsichord interjections
- Synthesiser **glissando** leads to Chorus that includes synthesised bells and a **picked** electric guitar
- Middle eight uses synthesiser **pad** sounds and descending **arpeggios**.

Material Girl

- 4/4, C major, 134 bpm
- Structure: Intro, Verse 1, Chorus, Intro, Verse 2, Chorus, Intro, Verse 3, Chorus, Chorus, Intro, Vocal Breakdown, Verse 4
- Verse 3 is sung half by the backing vocals and half by Madonna
- Verse 4 is sung half backing vocals and ad-libs – drums dropout
- Listen for Madonna's cries of ecstasy showing exuberance.

Crazy For You

- 4/4, E major, 96 bpm
- Structure: Intro, Verse 1, Chorus, Intro, Verse 2, Chorus, Intro, Chorus (with fade out)
- Noticeably slower than earlier tracks, opens with a I, IV, V **chord progression** and a synthesised marimba
- Half way through Verse 1 the mood is lifted by a synthesized **koto** effect
- Very wide **vocal range** – from low G♯ up to a high B (at the climax of the chorus)
- The final chorus includes ad-lib vocal ideas.

Into The Groove

- 4/4, C minor, 118 bpm
- Structure: Intro, Chorus, Verse 1, Chorus, Verse 2, Chorus, Middle Eight, Piano Solo, Middle Eight, Chorus, Chorus (changed vocal), Chorus (with fade out)
- Latin percussion: agogo bells and cabasa
- Spoken call to come out on the dancefloor
- Very nasal delivery of Chorus

- Verse is less energetic than Chorus
- Middle eight is built on two chords: G major and F major, with Madonna harmonising with herself in **3rds**
- The piano solo uses the C blues scale
- The penultimate Chorus has an alternate melody.

Live To Tell

- $\frac{4}{4}$, F major, 109 bpm
- Structure: Intro (two parts – second half is rhythm section), Verse 1, Chorus, Rhythm section intro, Verse 2, Chorus, Chorus, Link, Middle Eight, Instrumental link, Chorus, Chorus, Chorus (with fade out)
- Begins with no sense of pulse building up a **chord** of D minor 11
- Verse is built on chords of C major and G minor 7
- Chorus gets extra momentum from a pizzicato-effect synthesiser
- Listen for the **counter melody** in the **Middle Eight** and the end Choruses.

Papa Don't Preach

- $\frac{4}{4}$, F minor, 122 bpm
- Structure: Intro (strings then with rhythm section), Verse 1, Bridge, Chorus, Verse 2, Bridge, Chorus, Guitar Solo, Bridge, Chorus, Chorus, Chorus (with fade out)
- Classical string sound on synthesisers joined by rhythm section including cabasa
- Verse is in low vocal **register**
- Synthesised bell/piano answers the vocals in the Bridge
- Chorus is built with several short interlocking **motifs**.

Open Your Heart

- $\frac{4}{4}$, F major, 113 bpm
- Structure: Intro, Verse 1, Bridge, Chorus, Intro, Verse 2, Bridge, Chorus, Middle Eight, Intro (changed vocal) Bridge, Chorus, Coda (ad-lib vocal with fade out)
- Begins with **drum fill** and vocal exclamation
- Powerful rhythm section **groove**
- Verse uses hi-hat **fills** and is in low vocal range
- Bridge moves to the **dominant**
- Final Chorus has an ad-lib vocal line.

La Isla Bonita

- $\frac{4}{4}$, C# minor, 100 bpm
- Structure: Intro, Verse 1, Chorus, Instrumental Link, Verse 2, Chorus, Instrumental Link, Middle Eight, Verse 3 (synth cello melody for first half), Chorus, Chorus, Chorus
- Rhumba rhythm with two-bar chord pattern (C# minor to B major, C# minor)
- Chorus is built on **intervals** of a second
- Verse 3 is instrumental for the first half.

Like a Prayer

- 4/4, F major, 112 bpm
- Structure: Intro (spoken voice – choir – voice and organ – with rhythm section), Chorus, Verse 1, Chorus, Verse 2, Chorus, Modulation to minor key, Minor Verse 1, Chorus, Breakdown, Minor Verse 2, Chorus, Chorus (with fade out)
- Spoken intro has a **splashback** effect – **gospel choir** sing ascending three-note **motif**
- Latin percussion includes agogo bells and cowbell
- Chorus has additional hi-hat and a **polysynth** playing **quaver stabs**
- In third Chorus **gospel choir** comes to fore and there are additional percussion sounds: handclaps, vibraslap (chatterbox) and synthesised percussion
- Breakdown is built over a throbbing **pedal** note.

Express Yourself

- 4/4, G major, 114 bpm
- Structure: Intro, Chorus, Verse 1, Chorus, Verse 2, Chorus, Chorus Extension, Middle Eight, Chorus, Coda
- Opens with electronic percussion **loop**
- Backing vocals dropout when Madonna shouts 'Come on Girls'
- Chorus has frenetic **house-style** drums vocal in upper **register**
- Verse 1: Synthesiser **pans** from left to right.

Cherish

- 12/8, D major, 132 bpm
- Structure: Intro, Verse 1, Chorus, Verse 2, Chorus, Middle Eight, Solo, Verse 3, Chorus, Breakdown, Chorus (with fade out)
- Bouncy and optimistic, reminiscent of motown
- Chorus includes high synthesiser bells to support backing vocal
- Chorus 3 has **finger clicks** as does the Breakdown which also includes **tambourine**.

Vogue

- 4/4, A♭ major, 116 bpm
- Structure: Short spoken intro, Musical intro, Verse 1, Chorus, Verse 2, Chorus, Middle Eight, Chorus, Bridge, Rap section, Breakdown, Chorus, Coda (with spoken ending)
- **Bongo rhythm** similar to a salsa/samba **clave rhythm** – we also hear **agogo bells** (looped) given some sense of a Latin crossover
- Enigmatic **tonality** through the Introduction
- Orchestra stab signals verse, Vocal **stab** of 'vogue' in the second chorus
- **Semiquaver** snare fills dominate the drum patterns
- 'Get up on the dance floor' is the vocal climax with the voice at its highest and most intense

- **Rap** section uses chorus **backing track**
- Orchestra stabs return in the coda – song ends with Madonna speaking the title.

Justify My Love

- 4/4, F♯ minor, 99 bpm
- Structure: Intro, Verse 1, Chorus, Link, Verse 2, Chorus, Link, Middle Eight, Verse 3, Chorus, Coda (with fade out)
- Opens with very sparse **hip-hop** beat half way through a bar
- Verse 1 is spoken – low in voice and sensuous
- The first Chorus includes a **double-tracked** spoken vocal with the **hook** being the only thing sung.

Rescue Me

- 4/4, E♭ minor, 118 bpm
- Structure: Intro (sound effects – piano riff – voice), Verse 1, Chorus, Verse 2. Chorus, Middle Eight, Chorus (using Middle eight lyrics), Breakdown, Chorus, Rap, Chorus, Breakdown Chorus, Chorus (with fade out to FX)
- Opens with heartbeat merging into a tropical rainstorm – over synthesiser bass and sub-bass pattern is a synthesized panpipe **motif**
- Verse 1 is spoken
- Chorus has driving rhythm section and **double-tracked** lead vocal
- Middle eight begins with loud **orchestral stab** – lead vocal goes higher while backing vocals often move in **contrary motion**
- Breakdown features drums, percussion, bass and panpipe
- The fourth chorus includes **gospel-style** 'oohs' which are also heard in the fifth chorus 'Believe in the power'.

PUTTING BOTH ALBUMS INTO CONTEXT

In order to put both albums into context it is important that you have some knowledge of related albums. As well as other albums by the same performers you should try to listen to albums that influenced or were influenced by these albums, such as:

- *Rubber Soul* – The Beatles
- *Sgt Pepper's Lonely Hearts Club Band* – The Beatles
- *Songs in the Key of Life* – Stevie Wonder
- *Thriller* – Michael Jackson
- *Greatest Hits* – Sly and the Family Stone
- *Once Upon A Time* – Donna Summer.